Australians in Shanghai

T0298898

In the first half of the twentieth century, a diverse community of Australians settled in Shanghai. There they forged a 'China trade', circulating goods, people and ideas across the South China Sea, from Shanghai and Hong Kong to Sydney and Melbourne. This trade has been largely forgotten in contemporary Australia, where future economic ties trump historical memory when it comes to popular perceptions of China. After the First World War, Australians turned to Chinese treaty ports, fleeing poverty and unemployment, while others sought to 'save' China through missionary work and socialist ideas. Chinese Australians, disillusioned by Australian racism under the White Australia Policy, arrived to participate in Chinese nation building and ended up forging business empires which survive to this day.

This book follows the life trajectories of these Australians, providing a means by which we can address one of the pervading tensions of race, empire and nation in the twentieth century: the relationship between working-class aspirations for social mobility and the exclusionary and discriminatory practices of white settler societies.

Sophie Loy-Wilson is a Lecturer in Australian History at the University of Sydney.

Australians in Shanghai

Race, Rights and Nation in Treaty Port China

Sophie Loy-Wilson

Routledge
Taylor & Francis Group

LONDON AND NEW YORK

First published 2017
by Routledge

2 Park Square, Milton Park, Abingdon, Oxfordshire OX14 4RN
52 Vanderbilt Avenue, New York, NY 10017

Routledge is an imprint of the Taylor & Francis Group, an informa business

First issued in paperback 2019

British Library Cataloguing in Publication Data
A catalogue record for this book is available from the British Library

Library of Congress Cataloging in Publication Data
Names: Loy-Wilson, Sophie, author.
Title: Australians in Shanghai: race, rights and nation in treaty port
China / by Sophie Loy-Wilson.
Description: New York, NY: Routledge, 2016. | Includes bibliographical
references and index.
Identifiers: LCCN 2016013499| ISBN 9781138797628 (hardback) |
ISBN 9781315756998 (ebook)
Subjects: LCSH: Australians—China—Shanghai—History. | Australians—
China—Shanghai—Social conditions. | Shanghai (China)—Social
conditions. | Shanghai (China)—Race relations.
Classification: LCC DS796.S29 A96 2016 | DDC 305.82/
405113209041—dc23
LC record available at https://lccn.loc.gov/2016013499

ISBN: 978-1-138-79762-8 (hbk)
ISBN: 978-0-367-35040-6 (pbk)

Typeset in Galliard
by Keystroke, Neville Lodge, Tettenhall, Wolverhampton

To Judy and Kyle, for taking me with them
and to Muhilan, for finding a way

Contents

Figures

Preface and Acknowledgements

If the White Australia Policy has an afterlife, I came face-to-face with it in 1996. Flicking through a book on Shanghai's pre-communist architecture, *A Last Look: Western Architecture in Old Shanghai*, I first saw Daisy Kwok at the front of her family's now decrepit mansion in the Jing'an district of Shanghai. Standing on cracked cement and next to a clothes line, she wore a black velvet dress and white pearls. She must have been at least in her seventies. The caption told me that she was born in Australia but came to Shanghai in 1917 and that she identified as an 'Australian in Shanghai'. This struck me as unusual. Loosely schooled in the history of Australian diplomatic relations with China (I was brought up in embassies), I knew that Australia had not established formal diplomatic ties with China until the 1970s. Most of what I read on this history conjured up images of banquets and handshakes, leadership meetings and summits and the odd photograph of an Australian politician standing on the Great Wall. Nowhere in the visual canon of Sino-Australian relations had I encountered anyone like Daisy Kwok.

Now, twenty years on, I know that Daisy was a second generation Australian of Chinese descent who grew up in the Sydney suburb of Petersham before her father, George Kwok Bew, took the family to China, fleeing Australian racism and White Australia, on the one hand, and embracing Shanghai's famed modernity, on the other; he helped open the Wing On Department Store, now a Shanghai institution. Daisy was just one of many Australians who made lives in Shanghai between the wars. Their homes, workplaces, mission headquarters, nightclubs and dance halls are now sites of erasure, any evidence of an Australian connection long lost, or subsumed within the much larger presence of British 'Shanghailanders' in the city. Daisy herself stayed in China after 1949 and was persecuted and impoverished during the political campaigns of the 1960s. The image that so captivated me in *A Last Look* was taken in the 1980s when economic reforms in China had inspired nostalgia for Shanghai's capitalist past, and new respect for the men and women who remembered it.

Before Daisy died in 1990, she was finally given Australian citizenship, something she had been denied throughout her life. In the Australia of her birth, 'Asiatics' were undesirables, out of place in Australia's vision of itself as a white fortress in the British Empire. Overseas Chinese in other settler colonies faced the same laws.

This was a global history of racial exclusion illuminated recently by Marilyn Lake and Henry Reynolds in *Drawing the Global Colour Line: White Men's Countries and the Question of Racial Equality*. Chinese immigration restriction laws were in force in the Australian colonies from 1855, and subsequent iterations of these laws gradually denied Chinese arriving in Australia property rights and, after Federation in 1901, citizenship rights including voting rights, or rights to welfare. Daisy, the descendant of gold-rush era migrants, was one of many Australian-born Chinese who looked to Shanghai for a better future after the introduction of the Immigration Restriction Act or White Australia Policy in 1901, seeking opportunities not afforded them in the southernmost Dominion of the British imperial world.

Living in China in my teens, no one place more viscerally confronted me with empire's legacies than Shanghai. I first visited the city in 1997. Once Europe's premiere treaty port in Asia, Shanghai still bears the marks of its foreign concessions with a 'French town' modelled on Paris and a Bund lined with the old headquarters of the British elite – clubhouses, banks and hotels. When I first travelled there in my teens, I was in awe of the Art Deco grandeur of the Peace Hotel on the Bund, where every room was themed to differing national tastes (the Japanese room, the India room, the British room) and where an ageing jazz band from the 1930s still played in the bar. Later I was told by a Shanghai historian that before 1949 local Chinese were banned from using the hotel's main elevator which was then reserved for Europeans only. Chinese were forced to use the service elevator instead. The Bund was as much a reminder of European incursions into Chinese sovereignty as it was a dazzling evocation of a glamorous era.

Across the Bund, on the opposite side of the Huangpu River, a new district rose to meet the old one. Pudong was all sky rise and neon, with a TV tower turning pink and purple at night due to a light theme designed by a French expert. By the late 2000s, two buildings stretched the tallest: a Japanese bank with its controversial shape like a dagger sunk into the ground, and the Chinese Jingmao pagoda building, rising just over the Japanese sword hilt, and dubbed 'the latest symbol of China's rise'.

Leading off the Bund, facing away from Pudong, is Nanjing Shopping Street, the Pudong of the 1920s and 1930s. It was on this street that returned Chinese Australians built decadent department stores: Sincere, Wing On, Sun Sun and Da Sun – a story John Fitzgerald unearthed in *Big White Lie: Chinese Australians in White Australia*. These were the so-called four great companies, the harbingers of consumer capitalism on Chinese shores after the First World War. In my teens I was blind to this surprising Australian heritage at the heart of Shanghai's capitalist history. In my twenties I learnt of the fate of the Chinese Australian families who had sunk their money into the city at the height of its jazz era buzz. They lost their wealth, they went into exile in America, or they stayed. Many suffered. Some survived and ended up assisting Australian diplomats when they arrived in China after 'reform and opening' began, acting as cultural liaison officers, proof of a longer history of China–Australia relations prior to the cutting of ties after 1949.

I visited their decaying mansions on the edge of what was once the International Settlement. In rooms now inhabited by multiple families (following the redistribution of property in the 1950s), I saw glimpses of tarnished chandeliers and servants' quarters, cherub roof frescoes and ballroom dance floors. These mansions were lived in by Australians who were well connected between the wars, friends of the Republican era Kuo Min Tang government, despised by the many who fell through the cracks of that elitist, corrupt regime. These homes were the envy of the poorer, white Australians who arrived in Shanghai in such large numbers during the Great Depression looking for work, so much so that the British Government requested the Australian government ban all Australian migration to the city. More Australians came nonetheless and many left a mark in the archives of the Shanghai Municipal Police, a fact brought to my attention by Robert Bickers, historian of Shanghai par excellence, whose scholarship has long been my best guide to Shanghai's past.

Also on Nanjing Road, at the foot of the Chinese Australian department stores, marched student protesters and unionists in the 1920s, the men and women Richard Rigby wrote about so vividly in *The May 30th Movement*. May 30 refers to the shooting of Chinese protesters by British-led police in Shanghai's International Settlement on 30 May 1925, an event that shook China and caused an outburst of nationwide indignation and protest against British imperialism. In many cities from Beijing to Guangzhou, there were riots, strikes, boycotts and demonstrations, demanding not only compensation for the dead and wounded in Shanghai, but also a wholesale revision of China's foreign relations. In 2006, while starting research for a PhD thesis, I was rifling through Australia Union newspapers and was startled to find mention of the May 30th Movement in papers such as the *Labour Daily* and *One Big Union*. More research turned up correspondence between Chinese unionists and Australian unionists who saw commonalities of experience over labour rights and between Australia's and China's relationship to the British Empire. After all, as one Chinese unionist told an Australian he encountered in a May 30th protest in Hong Kong: 'Australia is like China, a nation oppressed by the British race. We have no quarrel with Australians, only with the British.'

What does it mean to identify as an Australian in China? Tackling this question in this book, I wanted to read Australian migration to China from a Chinese perspective, to show how being Australian in China provoked historical memories often forgotten in much of the future-focused rhetoric about Sino-Australian relations in China's economic boom years. This book is therefore about the origins of my own career as an historian. It is my attempt to understand the systems of knowledge of which I am a part, the traces they have left upon me, and the disparities which continue to characterise Australia's long encounter with China. It is thus doubly important that I acknowledge those who have helped me in the course of its development. I am grateful to the University of Sydney History Faculty, the National Library of Australia, the Australasian Pioneers Club, the Australian Historical Association CAL Bursary Program, the Alfred Deakin Research Institute, Deakin University History Faculty in Melbourne and, more recently, the Laureate Research Centre for International History in Sydney led by Professor Glenda Sluga, for funding various iterations of this project and for the confidence such funding inspires. I am similarly grateful for assistance from many librarians and archivists, but I would especially like to thank staff at Sydney's Mitchell Library, the National Library of Australia, the National Archives of Australia, the City of Sydney Archives, the State Records Office of New South Wales, the State Library of Victoria, the Shanghai Municipal Archives, the UK National Archives at Kew, the Singapore National Archives and the Hoover Institute at Stanford.

It wasn't until I started studying in the Department of History at the University of Sydney that I found the vocabulary to explore Australia's connections with China in a way that rang true for me, that accounted for the contradictory reactions my presence as an Australian in China provoked in people. I took classes with Kirsten McKenzie, who introduced me to a new kind of history which allowed historians to chart the spaces between national histories, *transnational* histories, as they were called. Kirsten is also a feminist historian, working with archival silences to bring the intimate and the political together, rewriting the histories of empire and governance in the process. She literally dwelt in the ruins of empires. In one of her lectures I learnt she had gained access to a secret black box in an old mansion in Lancashire built by the Lascelles family who made their fortune through sugar plantations and slavery in Barbados. In Kirsten I found a PhD supervisor who made seemingly marginal lives matter to the larger story and who was adept at untangling the reverberations and disruptions of migration and social aspiration in the colonial world. My associate supervisor at the University of Sydney, Chris Hilliard, brought me to the interwar period, to the complexities of class and to the great pleasures of British social and cultural history. Through Chris, I developed an interest in labour newspapers and working-class writing. This opened up the rich pickings of the Australian labour movement archive to me, leading me to uncover collections which would become indispensable as I battled to understand the strange, contradictory landscape of poverty and commercial modernity which characterised urban Australia between the wars.

At the University of Sydney, Ann Curthoys, Tamson Pietsch, Miranda Johnson, Glenda Sluga, Sheila Fitzpatrick, James Curran, Alison Bashford, Frances Clarke, Penny Russell, Richard White, Nicholas Eckstein, Chin Jou, Warwick Anderson, Shane White and Andres Rodriguez all provided advice and guidance: through teaching, scholarship or in person. Scholars from further afield such as Fiona Paisley, Sunil Amrith, Erez Manela, Heather Goodall, Julia Martinez and Ernest Koh provided helpful feedback at the early stages of my research. I would be remiss if I did not extend particular thanks to the vibrant postgraduate community in the Department of History at Sydney who tested and tightened so many aspects of my history writing. I thank Jennie Taylor, Hannah Forsyth, Briony Neilson, Elizabeth Todd, Samia Khatun, Alecia Simmonds, Jemima Mowbray, Michael Thompson, Nick Irving, Dave Earl, Agnieszka Sobocinska, Andy Kaladelfos and Chris Holdrige for their rich conversation and solidarity. Postgraduate colleagues from further afield – Kyle Harvey, Claire Lowrie and Nadia Rhook – were also exceedingly generous in this regard. I was lucky enough to spend a few months at the National Library of Australia on a Norman McCann Summer Fellowship alongside Andrew Thackray, Rebecca Saunders and Alexander Cameron-Smith, who all contributed their time and energy to discussing my project with me, often on long walks around Lake Burley-Griffin. My research on the history of Shanghai would not have been possible without the generous help of Robert Bickers, Isabella Jackson and Catherine Ladds. Through these historians I was exposed to new scholarship on Chinese treaty ports emerging from Bristol University's Chinese and Imperial History program. During my PhD candidature, I was lucky enough to attend workshops led by Tony Ballantyne and Antoinette Burton and am still benefiting from their insights into the instability and historical contingency of the modern political terms which we often take for granted: 'empire,' 'nation state', 'Chinese trade', 'European progress'.

Marilyn Lake has been a mentor throughout this project and her work has long influenced my own. Her ability to turn Australian history on its head, to see reverberations between Australia and America, Australia and China or Australia and the Pacific – connections rendered invisible in nationalist historiography – has opened up so many possibilities for exploring Australian lives in the world. I am extremely grateful for her support throughout my career and especially during the later stages of finishing this book, when I was living in Melbourne. While researching and lecturing at Deakin University, I was lucky enough to encounter: Kirstie Close-Barry, Sarah Pinto, Jonathan Ritchie, David Lowe, Sarah Paddle, Sue Chen, David Lee, Charlotte Greenhalgh, Clare Corbould, James Barry, Amit Sarwal, Billy Griffiths and David Walker, all of whom shaped the direction of my writing for this book. At the Laureate Research Centre for International History I could not have asked for better intellectual companions than Philippa Hetherington and Sarah Walsh. During the final stages of writing I presented my research at Wollongong University, National Technology University Singapore, the National University of Singapore, King's College London and Monash University. I am indebted to the History Faculty at these institutions for their feedback.

Numerous Chinese Australian historians and historians of the Overseas Chinese have shared their knowledge with me throughout the writing of this book. I would like to thank Kate Bagnall, Sophie Couchman, John Fitzgerald, Mei-fen Kuo, Paul Macgregor, Michael Williams, Mae Ngai, Henry Yu, Elizabeth Sinn, Evelyn Hu-deHart, Sascha Auerbach and Benjamin Mountford. I owe a special debt of gratitude to the many Chinese Australian descendants who warmly shared their archives and family histories with me. I would like to acknowledge the help of Paul and Maunie Kwok, Siaomen and Richard Horsburgh, Billy Fu, Brad Powe and Peter Hack.

Hannah Forsyth, Kirstie Close-Barry, Tamson Pietsch, Miranda Johnson, Anne Rees, Lachlan Strahan, Agnieszka Sobocinska, Mei-fen Kuo, Isabella Jackson and Andres Rodriguez have all read drafts of this book. In spite of having better things to do, you generously gave your time to reading parts of this manuscript when it was less than respectable. For its shortcomings, I remain responsible. My editorial team, Yong Ling Lam, Samantha Phua and Nicole Davis, were exemplary. I would also like to thank the anonymous reviewers for Routledge for their suggestions on drafts. Many others, now dispersed, have kept me company along the way. Kate Bower, Lexine Stapinski, Zoe Anderson and Sam Loy-Wilson provided much needed distraction. Jo Higgins hosted me in Singapore and Jennie Taylor and Simon Prince gave me a home in the UK. My grandmother, Norma Hardy, has supported me in many ways – intellectual and spiritual – and I would not have completed the book without her.

My deepest debt of appreciation is owed to my family. My parents, Kyle Wilson and Judy Loy, led me by the hand through an upbringing spent in Warsaw, Canberra, Moscow and Beijing, endlessly stoking my curiosity with books, journeys and ideas. My husband, Muhilan Sriravindrarajah, brought his special brand of positivity to every obstacle I faced. Knowing more than most what it means to manage multiple ethnic and national affiliations, he was often more excited by my work than I was and he never failed to rally me through his infectious enthusiasm and loyal encouragement. It is impossible to do justice to the gifts they have given me. This book is for the three of them.

Portions of this book were previously published as the following journal articles and are reprinted here with permission: 'White Cargo: Australian Residents, Trade and Colonialism in Shanghai between the Wars' in *History Australia*, 9 (3), pp. 154–177, copyright 2012 Monash University Press (all rights reserved, reprinted by permission); '"Liberating" Asia: Strikes and Protest in Sydney and Shanghai, 1920–39', in *History Workshop Journal*, 72, pp. 74–102, copyright 2011 Oxford University Press (all rights reserved, reprinted by permission).

Note on Chinese Language Use

The issue of correct naming across cultural boundaries is a painful one, and too often symptomatic of a wider incomprehension. The family that opens this book – the Kwoks – went by a number of names, the result of the Anglicisation of their surname during the process of immigration to the Australian colonies in the nineteenth century. Members of the Kwok family were variously known as the Kwoks, the Bews, the Gocks, the Gocksons, depending on the particular way in which their name had been Anglicised. When descendants have indicated their desire for me to use a certain form of the surname (in the case of Paul Gock, for example), I have respected their wishes. I have chosen to use the name Kwok throughout this book. Prior to the Second World War the Gocks Anglicised their Cantonese surname to Kwok. This was because their children were receiving a Western education and attending universities overseas and, additionally, Wing On had opened offices in San Francisco and New York. The Mandarin pronunciation is Kuo.

Similarly, the Anglicisation of the Chinese language across the nineteenth and twentieth centuries is reflected in my spelling of some city names and some surnames. These spellings reflect the context of the time. By the 1950s the Chinese language had changed again with the introduction of the simplified alphabet and new forms of Pinyin. Again, my use of this style of Chinese language is context-based and reflects the age in which my historical subjects found themselves.

I have mostly chosen to use the simplified Mandarin alphabet when representing the Chinese language sources that form a substantial part of this book. All translations are my own. When referencing Chinese-language primary source material from the Republican period, such as the *Global Half-Annual Journal* (*Huan Qiu Xun Kan*, 還球旬刊) or the *China Critic* (*Zhongguo pinglun zhoukan*, 中國評論周刊), I have used traditional Mandarin, in keeping with the usage at the time. I have used the same principle to represent Chinese place names, using Republican period terminology when necessary: so Chefoo for Yantai and Amoy for Xiamen.

Abbreviations

ACS	American Consulate of Shanghai
CoSA	City of Sydney Archives
HI	Hoover Institute
HKPRO	Hong Kong Public Records Office
KMT	Kuo Min Tang (government)
ML	Mitchell Library
NAA	National Archives of Australia
NCH	*North China Herald*
NLA	National Library of Australia
NSW	New South Wales
PRC	People's Republic of China
SFP	Shirley Fitzgerald papers
SLNSW	State Library of New South Wales
SLV	State Library of Victoria
SMA	Shanghai Municipal Archives
SMC	Shanghai Municipal Council
SMH	*Sydney Morning Herald*
SMP	Shanghai Municipal Police
SRNSW	State Records Office New South Wales
TNA	The National Archives of the UK
YMCA	Young Men's Christian Association
YWCA	Young Women's Christian Association

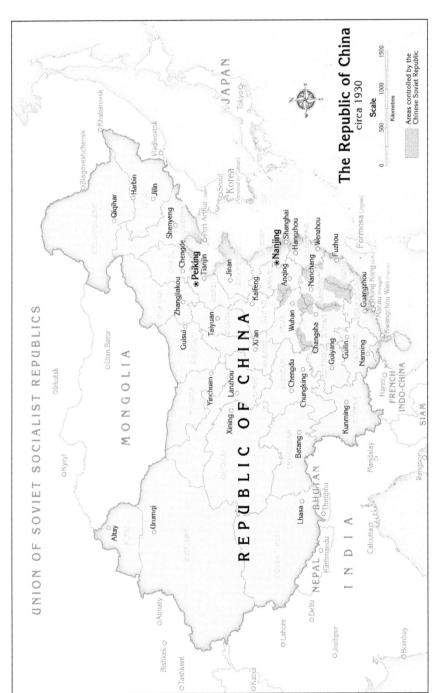

Map of China 1930

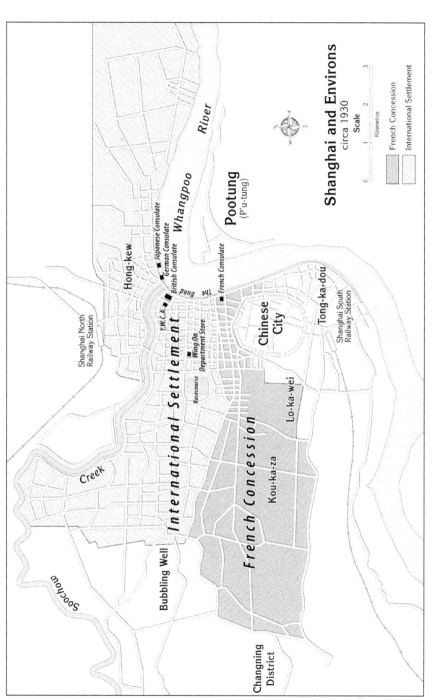

Map of treaty port Shanghai 1930

Introduction

In many ways this book began while I lived in Beijing with my parents in the 1990s, the era of reform and opening up inaugurated by Deng Xiaoping when he declared that 'poverty is not socialism, to be rich is glorious'. Our apartment was in the Australian Embassy, behind the Worker's Stadium, and not far by push-bike from the American Embassy. In May 1999, I rode into the midst of a student demonstration in the streets adjacent to the embassy. US warplanes taking part in the NATO bombing campaign in Yugoslavia had destroyed the Chinese Embassy in Belgrade, killing three and wounding twenty Chinese diplomats and journalists. Chinese students gathered outside the American Embassy to protest, holding banners denouncing American imperialism. As I entered the fray, I explained to those around me that I was Australian, not American. Taking in my Caucasian appearance, and T-shirt sporting a koala shaking hands with a panda, one bemused protester answered my pronouncements by observing that America and Australia were really one and the same. I mentioned something about Britain and the Commonwealth and he mentioned something about the Opium Wars and the ANZUS Treaty. Here I was, just another representative of the Western imperialists.

I probably shouldn't have viewed my Australian background as a way to ingratiate myself with Chinese student protesters. Australia in the late 1990s was in the midst of an anti-Asian immigration scare, when Pauline Hansen rose in Australia's parliament and announced that the nation was 'in danger of being swamped by Asians'. Her views, widely reported overseas, were often repeated back to me by Chinese friends at this time, curious to understand this surge of Australian racism towards Asian peoples. I explained that Australia had form in the area, dating back to the 'yellow peril' panics of the Gold Rush era and beyond. 'Ahh,' they replied, 'like America.'

Growing up as an Australian in China in the 1990s meant navigating a dense maze of historically situated stereotypes on both sides of the East/West divide about 'Westerners', 'foreigners', 'Asians' and 'Others'. How were Chinese perceptions of Australians made and circulated? What role did Australian views of China play in shaping these ideas? My attempts to answer these questions led me to cultural histories of Sino-Australian relations. Lachlan Strahan's *Australia's China* showed me how Australian lives in China were (and still are) inextricably tied to the history of Western imperialisms in Asia.[1] Australians were always viewed as the foot soldiers of greater forces, once the British Empire, by the 1990s the American Dream. In David Walker's *Anxious Nation*, I discovered that clichés of national character, expressed often through a casual racism, were as much part of my own past as they were embedded in Chinese history.[2] Australians, now thronging to Beijing as hopeful economic migrants, were perennially convinced that migration flowed too fast the other way, that a Chinese Empire would invade and storm 'our great White walls', to borrow Charles Price's evocative phrase.[3]

Disconnected histories

In some ways, we are all inheritors of the imperialisms which continue to shape the world around us: we are all 'haunted by Empire', as Anne Laura Stoler puts it.[4] When I began studying Australian history in my twenties, I found a conception of China tied to the legacies of the Gold Rushes and the White Australia Policy. Here was a Chineseness formulated when empire, Britishness and race purity were still sacred words for Australian colonists and when the exclusion of Chinese migrants was seen as fundamental to the preservation of a democratic Australia. Ann Curthoys calls this our 'uneasy' history:

> Our treatment of these Chinese men shames many of us, others perhaps find it understandable; in any event their treatment remains a matter of uneasiness. The Europeans thought these men barbarians, and the Chinese, in their turn, thought of the Europeans in the same way. In later decades, they would prove adept at managing the European society they encountered. Then we conjure a later image, of lonely Chinese men, after the rushes were over, working as market gardeners, growing and selling vegetables . . . These Chinese men perch at the edge of our historical consciousness, figures of fun and shame, a marker of colonial origins and the colonial vestiges in our present culture.[5]

For Curthoys, the point is this: Australians have long woven historical narratives around Chinese others and it is this storytelling, this weaving, which can tell us much about the kind of society we want to create, about how our ideas about rights and belonging are informed by racial anxieties and fragile nationalisms formed against the spectre of Asian outsiders. When I returned from China in the year 2000, I began to wonder how Australians in China fitted within this picture. If so much emphasis in Australian history was placed on Chinese *arriving in* or being *excluded from* Australia, what of Australians (including Chinese Australians) who travelled the other way? How did the Chinese respond to Australians in their midst? How do we write about Australia from a Chinese point of view?

In this study I address these questions in two ways. First, I use Chinese language sources to trace the lives of Australians in China between the wars: the First World War veterans, workers fleeing the Great Depression, merchants, missionaries, internationalists, socialists, diplomats. Second, I study the return

Figure I.1 Barker Street, The Rocks, 1900, showing the premises of Chinese
Australian companies Wing On & Co. and Wing Sang & Co.; Wing On
would eventually expand to Hong Kong and Shanghai. Views Taken
during Cleansing Operations, Quarantine Area, Sydney, 1900, Vol. II,
under the supervision of Mr George McCredie, F.I.A., NSW, State
Library of New South Wales a147122.

migration of a significant population of Chinese Australians to China after the
Chinese Revolution of 1911. Following in the footsteps of a new breed of Chinese
Australian historians, I take seriously 'the political activities, viewpoints and writings
of Chinese colonists themselves'.[6] I do so in the context of twentieth-century
Shanghai, a treaty port which attracted many Australians, spurred to migrate due
to the difficult economic conditions they faced after the First World War.

The presence of Australians in Shanghai in the interwar period triggered debate
in Chinese newspapers, left a mark on Shanghai police reports and also attracted
the attention of unionists, internationalists and anticolonial activists. For historians,
therefore, the interwar period provides rich archival pickings for the reconstruc-
tion of 'Australianess' through Chinese voices. 'Australia', as one Shanghai
journalist put it, 'was a country sustained on the agriculture of sheep', and was a
'British colony' populated by 'nothing more than prisoners'.[7] In this study I use
these sources to read Australian experiences of settler nation building in a Chinese

context. By rematerialising bodies of evidence that underscore the significance of China in a range of domains within the civic life of the Australian nation, including economics, class and labour, migration and citizenship and political rights and debates, I shed light on China's place in moulding the social patterns, cultural assumptions and political landscape of twentieth-century Australia. Further, by reconstructing Chinese Australian mentalities in treaty port Shanghai, I probe what these mentalities can tell us about Australia and empire from a Chinese point of view.

Ultimately, I argue that the existence of Chinese language archives about Australia provides a means by which I can address one of the pervading tensions of empire and nation in the twentieth century: the relationship between colonial and working-class aspirations for social mobility and the exclusionary and discriminatory practices of white settler societies. For when Australians went to Shanghai, and were forced to confront Chinese perceptions of the British Empire, they were in turn made to recalibrate their own investments in the imperial world. Australian national aspirations were fashioned and articulated in the context of these fraught contestations.

I do not attempt a comprehensive history of Australians in China. Rather, I focus specifically on unexpected patterns of migration and settlement which emerged in Shanghai in the first half of the twentieth century. The lives of Australians in Shanghai have left behind traces in repositories in Shanghai, Hong Kong, the United Kingdom, the United States, Sydney and Melbourne, and in the family archives of Chinese descendants scattered across Australia. The conflicted encounters of the individuals that I follow through these archives suggest that, at the very time Australia was involved in an immense nation-building project through racial exclusion known as the White Australia Policy, the country's economy was increasingly dependent on new markets in China. The resulting tension between economic imperatives and settler colonial nation building makes the interwar period a pivotal time in the history of Sino-Australian relations. Australian nation building coincided with migration and trade between Australia and China, and it occurred alongside attempts to control this spread of people and goods. The result was a clash between the borders valorised by nation builders and the chaotic mobility of individuals and commodities at the heart of the imperial order of things. This divergence – captured in the reverberations caused by Australians in Shanghai – helps make visible the weakening of the colonial order between the wars.

But even as this book emphasises the important place of China in the shaping and reshaping of Australia, it stresses that these engagements were, to quote Tony Ballantyne, 'not direct and simple encounters between two nations but rather enabled by institutions and structures that were rarely national in character'.[8] Instead, these forms of interdependence were the result of international trading and transport systems, the workings of imperial networks that fused together European, American and Japanese colonies, and the efforts of religious and internationalist groups (the Young Women's Christian Association, the International Workers of the World) to share knowledge on a global scale. Only by paying attention to the connections that linked Australia with other imperial sites in Asia, such as Shanghai, can we start to understand what these interdependences meant.

Australia in a Chinese context

It is now well established that the production of colonial knowledge occurred not only within the bounds of nation states and in relationship to their subject colonised populations, but also transnationally, across imperial centres. Marilyn Lake and Henry Reynolds's *Drawing the Global Colour Line* has shown how a racial lexicon forged in multiple colonial sites, especially the confrontational and violent sites of settler colonialism such as the Australian gold fields, shaped British and hence Euro/American conceptions of racial hierarchy.[9] Transnational histories have sought to break down simplistic distinctions between 'global', 'world' and 'national' histories by showing that global forces (networks, ideas, institutions, processes) do not 'transcend' nation states; they create them.[10]

My research seeks to contribute to the substantial body of scholarship which has emerged recently which aims to reconstruct the centrality of Asia in the making of Australian national culture. These works constitute what Tracey Banivanua-Mar has called 'counter histories', signalling a shift in Australian history away from British settler origins and towards a transnational frame of analysis that makes visible reciprocal flows of goods, people and ideas between Australia and other imperial sites in the Asia Pacific, including indigenous migration and motilities.[11] Such a frame contributes to the recovery of global connections that shaped how Australians measured and understood the link between race, rights and nationhood in the twentieth-century global landscape.

Importantly, these new histories construct Australia from the outside in, taking Asian sources about Australia seriously. Scholars of Australia's 'Top end' such as Julia Martinez, Adrian Vickers and Claire Lowrie have traced comparative colonial connections and forgotten migrations between Darwin and Singapore or Broome and Indonesia, while Devleena Ghosh, Heather Goodall and Samia Khatun have exposed the enmeshed world of Australia and the Indian Ocean.[12] Marilyn Lake, Tracey Banivanua-Mar, Warwick Anderson and Alison Bashford have found Pacific contexts foundational to the Australian production of colonial knowledge, while Fiona Paisley has looked to interwar internationalism and found Australian feminists deeply embroiled in debates over the rights of colonised peoples in the Asia Pacific.[13] For historians of Australian perceptions of Asia these new works impel us to reject sharp 'turning points' in Australia–Asia relations (the Fall of Singapore, for example) in favour of a new emphasis on the cultural and social forces gradually 'overturning' Australian antipathies to the region.[14]

But the field of Sino-Australia relations has been resistant to these trends. Either tilted towards a diplomatic approach anchored in the pivotal years following Australia's recognition of China in the 1970s, or focused primarily on the 'contributions' of white Australians to Chinese nation building in the Republican era, Sino-Australian scholarship has yet to grapple with Chinese 'agency' in the shaping of Australian civic life.[15] In contrast, Chinese Australian historians are breaking new ground in this regard, and this study takes up some of the directions suggested by their research. Mei-fen Kuo and John Fitzgerald have mined Chinese-language sources to reveal 'the richness of Chinese immigrant writing in Australian history and to better illustrate how these people believed they were taking part in a revolutionary movement towards a modern world', while Kate Bagnall has taken family history in a radical direction, tracing Chinese Australian return migration to villages in South China, and connecting distinct Chinese and English-language historiographies on these migrations in the process.[16] They have been assisted in this endeavour by the availability of Australia's large collection of Chinese-language newsprint, an archive Kuo wrote about extensively in *Making Chinese Australians: Urban Elites, Newspapers and the Formation of Chinese Australian Identity, 1892–1912.*

Following their lead, this book considers a fresh view of interwar Australian society as seen through sources produced in Shanghai. Doing so allows me to rethink Australian history in a Chinese context. The great debates over class and labour rights which echoed throughout Australia's interwar years were also connected to anticolonial protests in China, while economic hardship in Australia between the wars compelled many Australians to view China in a new light, as a frontier of economic opportunity and not the harbinger of yellow peril so familiar to Australians in the years around Federation.

This Chinese context also shifts our knowledge of Chinese Australian communities between the wars. What looks like a Chinese Australian population in crisis in the 1910s and 1920s — 'dying out' and 'almost extinct' as one Australian immigration official put it – appears more like a thriving community when Shanghai-based sources are taken into account. Nicole Ma, whose father lived in Sydney but worked in Shanghai for the Sincere Company, run by Chinese Australians, remembered: 'We were constantly on the move back then, constantly going between Sydney and Shanghai.'[17] Australian shipping companies were so dependent on Chinese Australian passengers for their Asia routes that they exhorted staff to prioritise Chinese customers: 'Pay these Australian-born Chinese all the attention you can, other lines are doing their utmost to cut into this important part of our revenue and we depend on our officers to assist in holding this . . . although these Chinese passengers give the appearance of being poor, many are wealthy.'[18] Following Chinese Australian lives beyond the bounds of the Australian nation reveals that empire and White Australia were not the major frames through which Chinese Australians reflected on the possibilities of their lives, within and outside of Australia. Angling their visions for the future towards Shanghai, many Chinese Australians negotiated racial exclusion through a series of overlaid familial, economic and political networks obscured in histories which overplay the role of White Australia in the shaping of Chinese Australian mentalities.

For their part, white Australians took the opportunity to move along networks made possible by Chinese Australians, and this mobility had consequences for Australian trade and foreign policy. By the mid-1930s, a series of Australian trade tours to China and Japan, conducted by the likes of steel magnate Essington

Lewis, Herbert Gepp, John Latham and scientist and internationalist Ian Clunies Ross, resulted in publications calling for urgent explorations of the East Asia trade if Australia's economy was to improve following the financial shocks of the interwar years.[19] These trade tours were facilitated by Chinese Australians who introduced Australian officials to their personal networks in China. After the First World War and the Great Depression, Australia could no longer depend on British imperial markets for its economic survival. In the interwar period, imperial withdrawal and revolutions in transportation forged connections between Australia and China exemplified by mobile Chinese Australians, who laid the foundations for a new kind of Australian encounter with Western imperialism in Asia. Therefore economic relations with China – already conducted so fluently by Chinese Australians – were at the forefront of Australian economic debate by the 1930s. Together these contrary tendencies began to unravel the ties that held the British imperial world together.

Outline

This book is about social and cultural connectedness between Australia and treaty port China in a sparsely researched period of Sino-Australian relations. It is not a diplomatic or institutional history; nor does it intervene in the key debates of Republican-era Chinese history. This is an Australian history written through China-based sources. It does not take up issues associated with Australia–Asia relations more broadly, such as Australian diplomatic and trade relations with Japan leading up to the Second World War; nor does it address the war at all, apart from fleetingly. Its focus is primarily treaty port Shanghai and it pays limited attention to Australians in other parts of China, such as Hong Kong or Chongqing. Thus it does not touch upon the fascinating world of the first Australian Consulate in China, headed by Frederic Egglestone and documented recently in the detailed work of William Sima, Kate Bagnall and Sophie Couchman.[20] It also does not address Australia's military presence in China during the Boxer Rebellion or the Republican period, and it neglects Jewish migration from Shanghai to Australia in the 1930s and 1940s, a story beautifully told by Chinese historian Antonia Finnane.[21] And finally, I do not address Australian communists or 'fellow travellers' who visited China after 1949 and wrote extensively about their experiences. Their stories have been given expert treatment in the work of Agnieszka Sobocinska.[22]

This study is largely concerned with figures who are non-canonical in both Australian and Chinese national history: Chinese Australian elites working closely with the KMT government, working-class Australians set adrift by the Great Depression, misfit Australians who found themselves in Shanghai police custody for a variety of reasons and Australian missionaries turned internationalists working in Shanghai's slum neighbourhoods. Individual Australians in Shanghai present a diverse picture. They came from all sorts of backgrounds, read material acquired from a variety of locations, and interpreted their place in Shanghai through events happening all over the world. They also stayed firmly planted, founding associations (the ANZAC Society, for example) and consolidating local connections. Thus there will be stories that do not fit easily into the broad patterns I detail, and lives that seem to swim against the dominant currents I identify.

The book begins in the 1910s, when Australian migration to Shanghai accelerated due to both the 1911 Chinese revolution and the aftermath of the First World War. Prominent Chinese Australian families opened businesses in Hong Kong and then in Shanghai. During the next few decades their lives would undergo a series of stark shifts impossible to predict when they first made the journey across the South China Sea from Sydney. Among the changes that buffeted them were the forces unleashed by the First World War, which would bring new kinds of global integration but also anxieties about foreign economic competition, resulting in the curtailment of free trade policies. In semi-colonial Shanghai, the signing of the Treaty of Versailles and the subsequent ceding of Chinese territory to Japan would cause anticolonial uprisings on a large scale, a story told by Erez Manela in *The Wilsonian Moment: Self-Determination and the International Origins of Anticolonial Nationalism*. The Second World War would bring even more radical change, beginning with the bombing of Shanghai by Japanese forces in 1937. Therefore, although it occasionally reaches beyond these dates, the main focus of this study is the period between 1914 and the outbreak of war in 1939.

Part I, 'Building empires, crossing borders', examines Chinese Australian return migration in the 1910s and follows the fate of these returnees after the Chinese Communist Revolution of 1949. It draws heavily on Chinese Australian family archives to tell a counter-history of White Australia, one less concerned with exclusion and more concerned with the opportunities provided by Sino-Australian trade and transport ties between the wars. Chinese Australians thrived in interwar Shanghai. Numbering among some of the most ardent supporters of the 1911 Chinese revolution, they were subsequently devoted nationalists and loyalists to Sun Yat Sen. Many returned after the introduction of a new Chinese nationality law in 1909 – the so-called 'law of bloodlines' – which declared that all children of Chinese fathers were automatically given Chinese citizenship no matter where they were born. Charting the reception of Chinese Australians in Shanghai across the twentieth century tells us much about the afterlife of the White Australia policy, the impacts of racial exclusion on non-white Australians and the cost of cultural assimilation under colonialism.

Part II, 'Finding work in the Eastern markets', goes on to explore the parallel movements of white Australian economic migrants into coastal China. It examines Chinese reactions in Shanghai to white Australian populations in that city fleeing poverty and unemployment in Australia during the Great Depression. In response to poor opportunities in the 1930s, out-of-work Australians travelled to Asian port cities in the thousands. Using the shipping routes previously carved out by Chinese Australian travel, these Australians saw Shanghai as an economic frontier, part of a European imperial web of which Australia was but one part.

Part III, '"Liberating" China, "saving" Australia', turns to the Australian trade unionists, missionaries and internationalists in Shanghai and their varied responses to the effects of Western imperial capitalism on China in the twentieth century. Using missionary and humanitarian networks sponsored by the Young Women's Christian Association, Australian unions held up Shanghai as an example of the humanitarian consequences of unregulated capitalism in colonial contexts. They used events in Shanghai such as the May 30th Movement to rally working-class Australians around a newly invigorated union cause during a time of sustained conservative government. Analysing interwar unionism and internationalism at this register reveals links between metropolitan Australian trade unions and Asian anticolonial protest movements left unacknowledged in Australian national histories.

In questioning the causal relationship between events in China and in Australian civic life, this study examines a set of issues that are central to the way we under-stand the history of Australian interactions with the Asian region. First, identifying the networks that connected Australia with treaty port China contributes to ongoing debates about the influence of Asia on Australian society. It traces the structures and practices which forged these networks, thus serving as a case study of the role Asia played in constituting the global connections that enabled, con-ditioned and regulated the hopes and experiences of Australians abroad in the period before the Second World War. Second, in expanding the boundaries of interwar Australian history to include Australian mobility to China, this book also provides a new context for conceiving of periodisation in Australian national history, one tied less to London and the British Empire and more to interconnec-tions within the Asia Pacific region. Third, as an examination of Chinese Australian mentalities through Chinese-language sources and family archives, this book opens up a little known part of Australian immigration history: return migration to China and the afterlife of the exclusionary practices which underpinned the White Australia Policy. Thus it deals with the texture and drama of the lives of people who experienced, at first hand, the world of White Australia and the birth and evolution of the Chinese Republic. In the process it evinces the need for historians to confront the historiographical and conceptual challenges posed by pasts that, although displaced onto territories now considered foreign, were once familiar.

When I struggled to explain my own national identity to Chinese student protesters in 1998 – insisting, as I did so, that being Australian was not the same as being British or American – I was one of a growing number of Australians reorienting their futures towards China. Here was a place once considered the antithesis of civilisation by many Australians, now transformed into an economic beacon for the hopes and dreams of a new generation. The destruction of the Belgrade consulate happened at a time of rising anti-Americanism in China, which was manifested, contradictorily, while many Chinese were also becoming enamoured of Western consumerism. During my Beijing years, state-run 'Friendship Stores' gave way to malls, Pizza Huts, McDonald's and Starbucks. Australian businesses such as Foster's Beer joined the rush of Western companies wooing Chinese consumers. I attended international school with the sons and daughters of the executives responsible for this wave. Later I taught 'American Business English' at Chinese universities.

Back home, globalisation was causing another set of Australians to look inwards, in the opposite direction. At the same time as I somewhat presumptuously joined a Chinese nationalist crowd in the condemnation of American imperialism, my own country was in the midst of yet another anti-Asian immigration scare and one that seemed familiar, repeating ongoing patterns of racial xenophobia dating back to the birth of Australian nationalism in the nineteenth century. The legacies of Western imperialism in Asia cast long shadows. If we are to develop a critical understanding of the inequalities currently fracturing a globalising world, one in which Australian living standards depend on decisions made in China not in London, these are the historical patterns and contradictions to which we need to pay close attention. For their history helped to establish uneven lines of global connection and irregular geographies of access that continue to condition immigration policy, racial attitudes and Sino-Australian relations today.

Notes

1 Lachlan Strahan, *Australia's Asia: Changing Perceptions from the 1930s to the 1990s* (Cambridge: Cambridge University Press, 1996).
2 David Walker, *Anxious Nation: Australia and the Rise of Asia, 1850–1939* (St. Lucia: University of Queensland Press, 1999).
3 Charles A. Price, *The Great White Walls Are Built: Restrictive Immigration to North America and Australasia* (Canberra: Australian Institute of International Affairs in association with Australian National University Press, 1974).
4 Ann Laura Stoler, 'Intimidations of Empire: Predicaments of the Tactile and Unseen', in Ann Laura Stoler (ed.) *Haunted by Empire: Geographies of Intimacy in North American History* (Durham, NC: Duke University Press, 2006).
5 Ann Curthoys, 'Men of All Nations, Except Chinamen: European and Chinese on the Goldfields of New South Wales', in Iain McCalman, Alexander Cook and Andrew Reeves (eds.) *Gold: Forgotten Histories and Lost Objects of Australia* (Cambridge, UK: Cambridge University Press, 2001), 103–104.
6 Marilyn Lake, 'The Chinese Empire Encounters the British Empire and Its "Colonial Dependencies": Melbourne, 1887', in Kate Bagnall and Sophie Couchman (eds.) Special Issue: Chinese Representations in Australia from the Mid-19th to the Early 20th Century, *Journal of the Chinese Overseas* 9.2 (2013): 178.
7 'Australia' (奧州), *Eastern Magazine* (*Dongfang Zhouzhi*, 東方周知) 31.2 (1935): 47.
8 Tony Ballantyne, *Webs of Empire: Locating New Zealand's Colonial Past* (Wellington: Bridget Williams Books, 2012), 22.
9 Marilyn Lake and Henry Reynolds, *Drawing the Global Colour Line: White Men's Countries and the Question of Racial Equality* (Melbourne: Cambridge University Press, 2008). See also: Sophie Loy-Wilson, 'New Directions in Chinese–Australian History', *History Australia* 11.3 (2014): 233–238; Kate Bagnall and Sophie Couchman (eds.) *Chinese Australians: Politics, Engagement and Resistance* (Leiden: Brill, 2015); John Fitzgerald, *Big White Lie: Chinese Australians in White Australia* (Sydney: University of NSW Press, 2006); Mei-fen Kuo, *Making Chinese Australians: Urban Elites, Newspapers and the Formation of Chinese Australian Identity, 1892–1912* (Melbourne: Monash University Press, 2013); Marilyn Lake, 'Chinese Colonists Assert Their Common Human Rights: Cosmopolitanism as Subject and Method in History', *Journal of World History* 21.3 (September 2010): 375–392; Peter Hobbins and Alison Bashford, 'Rewriting

Quarantine: Pacific History at Australia's Edge', *Australian Historical Studies* 46.3 (September 2015): 392–409.

10 Desley Deacon, Penny Russell and Angela Woollacott (eds.) *Transnational Ties: Australian Lives in the World* (Canberra: ANU ePress, 2008); Ann Curthoys and Marilyn Lake (eds.) *Connected Worlds: History in Transnational Perspective* (Canberra: ANU ePress, 2005), 7–10.

11 Tracey Banivanua-Mar, 'Shadowing Imperial Networks: Indigenous Mobility and Australia's Pacific Past', *Australian Historical Studies: Pacific Forum* 46.3 (2015): 340–355.

12 Julia Martinez and Adrian Vickers, *The Pearl Frontier: Indonesian Labor and Indigenous Encounters in Australia's Northern Trading Network* (Honolulu: Hawai'i University Press, 2015); Claire Lowrie, *Masters and Servants: Cultures of Empire in the Tropics* (Manchester: Manchester University Press, 2016) and 'White "Men" and Their Chinese "Boys": Sexuality, Masculinity and Colonial Power in Darwin and Singapore, 1880s–1930s', *History Australia* 10.1 (April 2013): 35–57; Devleena Ghosh, 'Under the Radar of Empire: Unregulated Travel in the Indian Ocean', *Journal of Social History* 45.2 (2015): 497–514; Heather Goodall and Devleena Ghosh, 'Beyond the "Poison of Prejudice": Indian and Australian Women Talk about the White Australia Policy', *History Australia* 12.1 (2015): 116–140; Samia Khatun, 'Camels, Ships, Trains: Translation across the "Indian Archipelago" 1860–1930', PhD Thesis, University of Sydney, 2012. See also: Regina Ganter, 'Editorial: Asians in Australian History', *Queensland Review* 6.2 (1999): i–iv; Regina Ganter, 'Turning the Map Upside Down', *Griffith Review* 9 Special Issue: Up North, Threats and Enchantment' (2005).

13 Marilyn Lake, 'Colonial Australia and the Asia-Pacific Region', in Alison Bashford and Stuart Macintyre (eds.) *The Cambridge History of Australia*, Vol. 1 (Melbourne: Cambridge University Press, 2013); Marilyn Lake, 'The Australian Dream of an Island Empire', *Australian Historical Studies: Pacific Forum* 46.3 (2015): 410–424; Warwick Anderson, 'Liberal Intellectuals as Pacific Supercargo: White Australian Masculinity and Racial Thought on the Border-Lands', *Australian Historical Studies: Pacific Forum* 46.3 (2015): 425–439; Tracey Banivanua-Mar, *Decolonising the Pacific: Indigenous Globalisation and the Ends of Empire* (Cambridge: Cambridge University Press, 2016); Hobbins and Bashford, 'Rewriting Quarantine', in David Armitage and Alison Bashford (eds.) *Pacific Histories: Ocean, Land and People* (Basingstoke: Palgrave Macmillan, 2014); Fiona Paisley, *Glamour in the Pacific: Cultural Internationalism and Race Politics in the Women's Pan-Pacific* (Honolulu: University of Hawai'i Press, 2009).

14 Agnieszska Sobocinska, 'Overturning the Point: Exploring Change in Australia–Asia Relations', *History Compass* 12.8 (2014): 642–650, and *Visiting the Neighbors: Australians in Asia* (Sydney: University of New South Wales Press, 2015).

15 James Reilly and Jingdong Yuan (eds.) *Australia and China at 40* (Sydney: University of NSW Press, 2012); Peter Thompson, *Shanghai Fury: Australian Heroes of Revolutionary China* (Sydney: William Heinemann Australia, 2012); Craig Collie, *The Reporter and the Chinese Warlords* (Sydney: Allen & Unwin, 2013).

16 Kuo, *Making Chinese Australians*, 1; Fitzgerald, *Big White Lie*; Kate Bagnall, 'Rewriting the History of Chinese Families in Nineteenth-Century Australia', *Australian Historical Studies* 42.1 (March 2011): 62–77.

17 Phone conversation with Nicole, descendant of Ma Ying Piu of the Sincere Corporation, 15 December 2015.

18 As an E&A circular explained: 'The presence of the Chinese crews brought an unexpected benefit to the E&A ships. The Chinese families living in Australia usually chose an E&A ship to take them to Hong Kong when they visited their relatives for a holiday and a sizable deck passenger trade was developed. Although

these Chinese passengers often gave the appearance of being poor, many were wealthy market gardeners enjoying a well earned rest.' G. A. Hardwick, 'A Century of Service: The Eastern and Australian Steamship Company Limited', *Journal of the Royal Australian Historical Society* 66.2 (September 1980): 96.

19 Ian Clunies Ross (ed.), *Australia and the Far East: Diplomatic and Trade Relations* (Sydney: Angus & Robertson in conjunction with the Australian Institute of International Affairs, 1936) and especially chapter five by H. D. Black, Lecturer in Economics at the University of Sydney, 'China as a Possible Market for Australian Production', 243–284; A. C. V. Melbourne, *Report on Australian Intercourse with Japan and China, Submitted to the Senate of the University of Queensland by ACV Melbourne* (Brisbane: Government Printer, 1932).

20 Will Sima, *China and ANU: Diplomats, Adventurers, Scholars* (Canberra: Australian National University Press, 2015); Kate Bagnall and Sophie Couchman (eds.) *The Chungking Legation: Australia's Diplomatic Mission in Wartime China* (Canberra: Department of Foreign Affairs and Trade and the Chinese Museum, 2015). See also: Warren G. Osmand, *Frederic Eggleston: An Intellectual in Australian Politics* (Sydney: Allen & Unwin, 1985).

21 Antonia Finnane, *Far from Where? Jewish Journeys to Shanghai* (Carlton: Melbourne University Press, 1999).

22 Agnieszka Sobocinska, 'Visiting the Neighbours: The Political Meanings of Australian Travel to Cold War Asia', *Australian Historical Studies* 44.3 (2013): 382–404.

Part I

Building Empires, Crossing Borders

1 The Kwok Family in Treaty Port China, 1880–1949

Shanghai was neither Daisy's birthplace nor her native home. By 1949 most of her brothers and sisters had left together with their families. But Daisy remained.[1]

Chen Danyan, *Shanghai Princess* (陈丹燕著，上海的金枝玉叶)

(Taibei Shi: Erya chubanshe, 1999), 15

I would again point to the necessity of sending to China a commission or a High Commissioner with diplomatic rank to inquire into the conditions of the China trade. There seems to be a complete misconception in Australia of the importance of the China market. I enclose to you a picture of a new department store which has just been opened in Shanghai under the direction of Australian trained Chinese . . . This is only one of a number of these department stores.[2]

George Ernest Morrison to W. A. Watt, Head of the Melbourne Chamber of Commerce, Peking, 17 September 1918

At the end of the Pacific War, hundreds of thousands of people were uprooted with the expansion of the Japanese Empire across the Pacific.[3] The Japanese Army occupied the Shanghai International Settlement in December 1941. Over the next three years Allied citizens living in the city were gradually placed under house arrest and then forced by the Japanese Army into internment camps.[4] In 1945 the Swiss consul general toured these camps on behalf of the Australian government to compile detailed lists of internees needing repatriation and assistance from the Red Cross.[5] One section of the internee population proved especially hard to categorise – internees claiming to be 'bona fide' Australians and yet of Chinese appearance.[6] This group held paperwork which showed that they were Australian citizens; yet, upon visual assessment, they were patently of 'Chinese origin'.[7] Anxious to provide clarity in tense and chaotic circumstances, the Swiss consul general pushed this group of internees for more information: where were you born and to whom? How did you come to be in Shanghai? Are you Chinese? Are you Australian?[8]

The Swiss consul general's detailed list is one of the few known documents testifying to the existence of a small yet prominent community of Australian-born Chinese who built lives in Shanghai in the first half of the twentieth century.[9] There they formed a unique set of families, travelling frequently between Australia and China, until 1949 when 'frontiers slammed shut' after the Chinese Communist Party banned emigration and imposed strict entry/exit controls on the movement of people and capital.[10] While scholars have established that Australia's Chinese population declined sharply in the first half of the twentieth century, few have interrogated why this might be or where Chinese Australians went next. Drops in Chinese Australian population figures have, in the past, been explained using vocabulary also applied to Indigenous Australians; Chinese Australians were 'in decline' or 'dying out'.[11]

This prevailing view of Chinese Australians was reflected in a conversation between Chinese Australian activist William Liu and a member of the staff of the Minister for Home and Territories in Melbourne in the late 1930s, as reported by Liu:

> I was talking to one of the staff and . . . he said there would be no more Chinese in Australia by the 1940s because of the Immigration Restriction Act. The old timers were dying, few new Chinese migrants were allowed in, there were very few women and a handful of children being born. I told him 'It looks like Australia is going to do the same to us Chinese as it did to the Tasmanian Aborigine.'[12]

Some in the Chinese community shared this view. In 1939 the manager of Wing On & Co. in Sydney wrote to Chiang Kai-shek, the leader of the Chinese Republican government, to ask him to intervene with the British government to allow more Chinese people to enter Australia. He did this because he feared that, 'apart from the native [Australian] born, the majority are old and weak'.[13]

But while white Australians and some resident Chinese Australians may have imagined Chinese Australians as a 'dying race' after 1901, the view from China tells a different story. An average of 9,000 Australian-born Chinese departed Australia every five years between 1915 and 1939, and many had their sights set on two of Asia's biggest treaty port cities: Hong Kong and Shanghai. Here they were part of a larger domestic Chinese migration from rural to urban areas.[14] In Shanghai, Chinese Australians joined over a million rural Chinese migrants attracted by China's pre-eminent 'city of immigrants'.[15] If London was where Anglo-Australians went to 'seek their fortune', then Shanghai was the 'metropole' of the Chinese Australian world.[16]

Chinese Australians thrived in Shanghai in the interwar decades after Sun Yat Sen invited them to return and 'help build the Chinese nation'.[17] They numbered among some of the most ardent supporters of the 1911 Chinese revolution and were subsequently devoted nationalists and loyalists to Sun Yat Sen.[18] Descended from goldrush-era immigrants who settled in Australia in the nineteenth century, Shanghai's Chinese Australians were typically second- or third-generation Australians and well equipped to navigate the semi-colonial society they encountered in China's treaty ports. Usually converted Christians and highly educated, many spoke English as a first language. 'We had English-speaking Australian

Figure 1.1 Chinese Australians in Shanghai, 1931. Back (left to right): Arthur
Wong; Arthur's wife, Violet Mary; Ruby Fay; Mary (Ernest's wife);
Alfred's wife, Eileen Fay; Thelma Fay (eleven years old); Ernest Wong;
Rosy Wong. Front (left to right): Harry Fay Jnr (three years old),
Mr Wong Chee (Wong Hoong Narn).

Source: Marina Mar (née Fay) via Chinese Australia Historical Images in Australia website,
call number: 0166_23001.

servants in Sydney,' Daisy Kwok remembered, 'and Chinese language was banned
in our home anyway lest it ruin our accents'.[19] Many Chinese Australians were
Eurasian and some had 'wives of European origin'.[20] In 1945 the Swiss consul
general interviewed a Eurasian called 'Luther James Lismore Yung', 'Accountant
– Australian of "Chinese origin",' who was born in his namesake of Lismore in
1895 and married to Alice Yuin Ding Young, from the same town. The consul
general also met the Gwok-gew sisters, Gwendoline Iris and Ann Muriel, born in
Sydney in 1915 and 1910. Efigenia Quark, although born Eurasian in Peru, had
Australian citizenship because she was married to Frank William Quark from
Bundaberg, Queensland. Edith M. E. Kwok, born in London, had become
Australian through her marriage to Tai Chiu Kwok from Sydney. Their children
had no passports, having been born in Shanghai, haven to the stateless, where,
famously, a passport was not required.[21]

In company with the Swiss consul general, governments and historians have
struggled to categorise Chinese Australians. In fact, the group is rarely visible in
state archives because the complex forms of geographical mobility and cultural

Figure 1.2 Chinese Australians at a Shanghai garden party, 1934. Left to right: Alice Yung; Gladys Janne; Alice and Luther's daughter, Jessie; Australian-born journalist Vivian Yung Chow; and his brother Luther Yung.

Source: Private Collection of Brad Powe.

exchange that they inherited sat uncomfortably with state-produced ideas about belonging and citizenship. Once they returned to China, the reach of their transnational lives was lost in loose categorisations. In the Republican and Socialist periods they were grouped under the title 'Returned Overseas Chinese' (*guiguo huaqiao*), while in twentieth-century Australia they were described as having been 'repatriated' or 'returned to their native land'.[22] In the legal nomenclature of the White Australia Policy some Australian-born Chinese were called 'naturalised Chinese' or carriers of CEDT (Certificates of Exemption from the Dictation Test). Eurasian journalist Vivian Yung Chow preferred the term 'Australian-born Chinese'.[23] In Sydney – forty years after the Swiss consul general compiled his list – Chinese Australian historian Mavis Gock Ming, a friend of Daisy's while they were both in Shanghai, reflecting on her childhood in Perth, her adolescence in 1930s Shanghai, her adulthood in socialist Beijing and her retirement in Sydney, also tried her hand at giving the community a name and came to the following conclusion: 'I wonder if being Chinese is [really] something that can be measured at all.'[24]

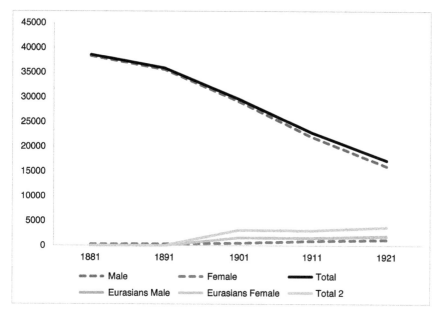

Figure 1.3 Chinese population of Australia, 1881–1921.

Source: Australian Bureau of Statistics.

Reading Chinese Australian journeys to Shanghai

Little is known about Shanghai's Chinese Australians. As their life stories are typically subsumed into the history of a much larger group of émigrés – the returned overseas Chinese in Shanghai – they have not featured in Chinese language histories or in scholarship in the West. While there is a growing body of academic and popular history drawing attention to white Australian experiences in Shanghai, epitomised by Peter Thompson's *Shanghai Fury: Australian Heroes of Revolutionary China,* the history of returned Chinese Australians in China remains little researched.[25] The information we do have documents their history up until the 'watershed' year of 1949, when the severing of ties between the two countries cut some families in half, closing off communication between Chinese Australians who left Shanghai before 1949 and those that chose to stay behind in the city.[26] For those who stayed, their Australian connections were obscured by the inflated dichotomies of 'East/West' or 'communist/free', mythologised during the Cold War. The overdetermination of 1949 as a year of 'radical break' in Australia–China relations has meant that historians have rarely ventured across the 1949 divide to trace Chinese Australian lives.[27]

This chapter emphasises a type of continuity in China–Australia relations by telling the story of Chinese Australians in Shanghai in the first half of the twentieth century. It does so by following the life of Daisy Kwok, who arrived in Shanghai from Sydney in 1917 during the heyday of Chinese Australian travel to that city and stayed after the communist takeover in 1949. Having survived imprisonment and persecution during the Cultural Revolution, Daisy died in Shanghai in 1998 as an Australian citizen; the Australian government reissued her Australian passport at an official ceremony held at the Australian consulate in Shanghai in 1989.[28] Bilingual, highly educated and a gifted chronicler of the Chinese Australian connections that had so deeply affected her life, she greatly assisted staff at the Australian consulate when it reopened in Shanghai in 1987 – translating documents, teaching Chinese language and as a repository of a longer history of China–Australia connections prior to the cutting of diplomatic ties in the 1950s.

Although Daisy began writing her memoirs in 1989, she never finished them. Her family asked Chinese author Chen Danyan to compile and complete her manuscripts. These were published posthumously as ＇上海的金枝玉叶＇ (*Shanghai de Jin zhe Yu ye*), or 'Shanghai's jade twig, golden leaf', and quickly made the bestseller lists in China.[29] Mavis Gock Ming translated the memoirs into English with the help of Daisy's son, and titled the English-language version *Shanghai Princess: Her Survival with Pride and Dignity*.[30] Mavis's own life had moved in step with Daisy's. They had played together as children and suffered similar fates during the Cultural Revolution. As a fellow Gock from the same village, her father had worked for Daisy's father in Shanghai in the 1930s, and Mavis also chose to stay in China after 1949.

In order to tell Daisy's story, I rely on four sets of sources: Daisy's published memoirs as they appear in the Chinese-language version of *Shanghai Princess*; files from the Australian Department of External Affairs; interviews conducted with Daisy's friends and family; and the numerous personal archives of Chinese Australian families shared with me by their descendants. These family stories make up an archive of fragmentary, often nostalgic memory.[31] There are personal stories of emotional attachments within and beyond families but, at the same time, there are histories of Shanghai's connections with Australia, of migration, of failed migration under the White Australia Policy, of the development of business and trading networks, of religious conversion and cultural exchange.[32] What becomes clear when these family stories are placed against state-based archives (immigration records, passports, consular files, internment records) is the complex interplay of assimilation, adoption, separation and conflict that found their way into the family histories, while being flattened out in institutional records.

Since this adaptive syncretism was anything but the deliberate policy of a White Australia, which depended on the maintenance of social and racial difference, the lives of second- or third-generation Chinese Australians sit uncomfortably within readings of Australian history which figure them as victims of colonial rule or marginalised minority within the Australian state. Chinese Australians were not 'natives of Shanghai', nor were they colonised peoples of Australia; they were aspirational migrants drawn to Shanghai through entwined networks of family and capital. Their very existence spoke to the imperfect reach of settler colonial forms of governance and population control. That a significant population of mobile

Chinese Australians maintained family ties between Australia and China in the first half of the twentieth century (the apogee of White Australia) testifies to the partial failure of the race-based population management favoured by Australian colonial governments since the 1850s.[33] As we shall see, Chinese Australians were both the beneficiaries *and* the victims of the imperial governance systems some of them learnt to evade so well. Many of the family histories explored here were marked indelibly by the Cultural Revolution, when the complex foreign ties of overseas Chinese, once so beneficial, became grounds for persecution.

How do we read Chinese Australian journeys to Shanghai across the long twentieth century? Drawing on what Nancy Green has called the 'mezzo level' of comparison between 'regions, cities and nations', I read these journeys as part of a back and forth between the politics of the local, the national and the transnational in order to recognise networks between different political cultures and different levels of governance (family, company, government, empire).[34] I use this comparative frame to question narratives of Asian immigration to Australia that view such movements solely through the lens of imperial power and restriction. While the White Australia Policy certainly contributed to the globally comparative political consciousness of the Australian-born Chinese world, it had an unstable and contingent power over their lives once in Shanghai.[35] Viewing Chinese Australian lives within and outside of White Australia – in semi-colonial *and* socialist Shanghai – gives us a better chance of understanding how seemingly conflicting activities fit together to produce and sustain a series of (never ironclad and always unstable) transnational connections between Australia and Asian treaty ports like Shanghai. These connections often lasted for lengthy periods and produced, in many instances, enormous profits for Chinese Australian businesses, even while they were also shaped by various power regimes with a perennial need to shore themselves up and to seek tighter control.

Daisy Kwok's Shanghai 1909–1949

Daisy Kwok was born in Sydney's Chinatown on 2 April 1909, the seventh child of George Kwok Bew and Darling Bew.[36] While her father had arrived in Australia in the 1880s as a gold miner, her mother was Australian-born Chinese – named Darling because she was the first Chinese girl born near the Darling River.[37] George Kwok Bew had gained naturalisation in Fiji in 1903. Like most Chinese Australians, George and Darling were Cantonese, and their families came from neighbouring villages in Zhongshan near the Pearl River Delta.[38] They had met at the home of a Christian minister in Sydney, John Young Way, who also acted as Darling's guardian.[39] She was sixteen when she married George Kwok Bew.[40] The couple settled in Sydney, where George worked as a market gardener and then at the Wing Sang & Co. grocery store, managed by James Gocklock and Philip Gockchin, two men who also came from the same village as Kwok Bew.[41] Their timing was fortuitous. Archives of the Chinese consul general of Singapore, who visited Australia in 1902, confirmed that the largest Chinese Australian communities were to be found in Sydney and Melbourne, so there were plenty of customers for the new business.[42] Wing On (formerly Wing Sang) thrived and George Kwok Bew moved his family of eight to a sprawling homestead in Sydney's suburbs with rose gardens, lush parlour rooms, long verandahs and white Australian servants. Daisy remembered it clearly:

> I was eight years old when we left Australia, but I still had a vivid memory of the house . . . Breakfast and lunch were eaten in the kitchen, but dinner was served in the dining room. As a rule we ate western food, as our maid was Australian.[43]

George Kwok Bew made sure his family followed the rituals of middle-class life becoming of Australian families of their class; they went to the opera, to church and to Sunday school. Chinese was banned in the home and the children were brought up speaking only English. And yet wealth and assimilation could not insulate the children from racism: 'there was much racial discrimination in school . . . the children at Sunday school called me all sorts of names, so I decided not to go there again'.[44]

Not all Chinese Australian families lived like the Kwok Bews. Mavis Gock Ming's father, Willy Gock Ming, also worked in a family-run grocery store (Wing Hing & Co. in Perth), but it was not as successful. In 1910 he married his English teacher, Mabel Jenkins, a Christian who taught English to Chinese market gardeners as part of her mission work. Their interracial marriage meant that their church congregation and Mabel's parents cut contact with the couple. Mabel gave birth to Mavis, the second of five children, in 1916. Although the family was not destitute, there were no trips to the opera and certainly no servants. Mabel felt 'outside of' white society, and her brother Harry recalls the racist taunts they received: 'The opportunity to mix with the wider community was not great.' Like the Kwok Bew children, the Ming children always spoke English at home: 'They never spoke Chinese. Their Dad had tried to teach them some expressions but they only picked up a few words.'[45]

In 1917 George Kwok Bew moved his family back to China and chose to settle in Shanghai, far away from his native village in Guangdong, so that he could manage the newly opened Wing On Department Store in the city's International Settlement. Immigration records show that members of the family were already frequent travellers; they went to Hong Kong three times before 1910.[46] Shanghai, however, with its maze of foreign concessions and laws around extraterritoriality, rendered them foreigners. It was so far removed from Daisy's world that she told her classmates in Sydney that Shanghai was a restaurant, not a city.[47] George Kwok Bew's decision to move his family there was motivated by a combination of patriotism and business sense. Like many Chinese Australians, Kwok Bew was frustrated by the restrictions placed on Chinese Australians by the White Australia Policy.[48] In Sydney, anti-Chinese racism was damaging his ability to work in the fruit and vegetable business. The formation of anti-Chinese leagues in most of Australia's main cities in the 1900s continued to stifle an 'atmosphere of liberty and free commercialism'.[49] George Kwok Bew claimed that, due to the activities of the anti-Chinese leagues, the value of his business at Sydney's Belmore Markets fell from £4,000 in 1903 to £1,000 in 1905.[50] Mei-fen Kuo has suggested that other factors also played a role in Kwok Bew's decision. He had successfully collected shares for the Wing On company as early as 1916 and had impressed Wing On proprietors in the process.

Commercial success in Shanghai and the expansion of the Wing On business empire represented a form of resistance to the racial ideas that underwrote both immigration restriction in Australia and British imperial incursion into Chinese sovereignty. Shanghai was also the safest place to invest in Republican China. For those who preferred to keep their money safe, Hong Kong and Shanghai were favoured refuges from the insecurity and corruption of Republican China. Many *huaqiao* chose to settle in these places, or perhaps their county capital or Canton, for family reasons as well as in order to protect their investments.[51] In Shanghai, the Wing On Department Store would form a base from which to move goods and capital along established British maritime trade routes through Oceania and East Asia; train Chinese personnel in modern manufacturing and business management; develop social and business networks; and introduce, in John Fitzgerald's words, a 'new style of commercial egalitarianism to China'.[52] Wing On would be a Chinese-owned company for Chinese customers operating in direct competition with the many European, Japanese and American businesses that dominated the city.

The Kwok Bews travelled for six weeks between 1917 and 1918 on board the *Nankin*, passing through Manila and Hong Kong on the journey. In Manila their eldest daughter, Edie, met her future husband, Chiu Tsing-fang, a diplomat at the Chinese Embassy.[53] Life on the ship was instructive for the young family, as it served as a model for Asian treaty port life more generally, where distinctions of class and race jostled uncomfortably against each other, causing confusion and social censure, but also offering opportunity. While the Kwok Bews could afford to travel first class, white Australians on the same route often chose to travel second class, especially after the onset of economic depression in Australia in the late 1920s. Clarrie Phillips and his wife Doss, who were from rural Victoria, travelled second class on the *Nankin*, leading their friend, Jim Pettigrew, a ship's officer, to avoid them socially. As Clarrie's brother Rex, a Shanghai resident, explained in a letter:

> A white man or woman cannot travel around Eastern ports second class on these ratty little boats and expect to retain the dignity and prestige of the white man in the East . . . Jim is anything but a snob but he is a ship's officer and ship's law demands that they travel and associate with saloon passengers.[54]

As Chinese Australians were regulars on the Eastern shipping lines, they were often more aware of these subtleties than white Australians. By the 1920s Chinese Australians were so important to shipping lines in the Far East that companies like E&A (Eastern & Australian Steamship Co.) began to specifically target luxury journeys at Chinese Australian customers in their marketing literature.[55]

Rather than reifying rigid categories of race and empire or the dichotomous agendas of oppressed Chinese and controlling colonists, the divergent experiences of some white Australians and Chinese Australians on ships show the steam passage from Australia to the East as a crucible in which the geographical, social and semantic alloy of Australian colonial relations could be resmelted.[56]

Far from placing white Australians within an imperial universe, travelling to Asian treaty ports introduced both white and Chinese Australians to a world system in which Australia was marginal and Australian claims to whiteness tenuous and unstable. While Australians were not counted separately in the Shanghai census but bracketed with the British, they were often excluded from British social institutions and clubs and looked down on as 'stablehands' and 'colonials'.[57] The Shanghai Club, in Lachlan Strahan's words, 'was for the more pukka English who looked down on Australians, even Anglophiles, as uncouth colonials, and they expressed their superiority in patronising comments'.[58] Their arrival in Shanghai would only exacerbate this sense of social chaos. Confronted with the lower-class white Australians who travelled second class on the ship and often peopled the boarding houses close to the docks, many Australian émigrés in Shanghai chose to quickly identify as English, a practice that the ANZAC Society of Shanghai bitterly condemned: 'There is a certain class of young Australian and New Zealander who secures a comparatively good position with a local firm and then tries to pretend that he is an Englishman. This has been one of our great difficulties in Shanghai.'[59]

Class dynamics could often trump race when it came to inclusion and exclusion. In November 1947 two Australian warships, HMAS *Australia* and HMAS *Bataan*, visited Shanghai. A strict hierarchy governed shore leave: 'the officers were accorded temporary membership of the prestigious clubs, including the Shanghai, French and country clubs, while ratings had to be content with the Union Jack and US Army Clubs'.[60] Even those who were given privileges and access to the best clubs could experience some of this social exclusion. Australia's Trade Commissioner in Shanghai (1935–1941), Ivor Bowden, was given access to the Shanghai Club but rarely went there. His son Ivor believed that his father 'saw himself and was seen by others as Australian'.[61] Many Australians felt an affinity with their fellow white colonials from Canada. Canadians celebrated Christmas 1942 with the Australian diplomats.[62]

Chinese Australians, on the other hand, entered a new social world in which their status and influence were linked to the success of prominent Chinese Australian businesses in the city. After arriving in Shanghai, the Kwok Bews were quickly ensconced in one of the best hotels in Shanghai – the Dung Ya Hotel – managed by the relations of Darling Bew who also worked for the Sincere Department Store:

> Our Uncle Gocklock, whose first wife was my mother's sister, also lived in the same hotel. He was to be the managing director of the new Wing On company with my Father. He had a Ford car which was considered very luxurious in those days.[63]

The association with Wing On would make them minor celebrities, with Kwok family christenings, weddings and funerals reported in the *North China Herald*. For Chinese Australian journalist Vivian Yung Chow, the visibility of Chinese Australian businesses in Shanghai marked the community as separate from Shanghai locals. The 'Australians', as he called them, had shown everyone in China that they were the most forward looking, unassuming and practical people of Chinese descent the world over: 'The world can see how true this is by a visit to Shanghai. They note the difference between the Australian Chinese department stores and the "home side" at business. There is no comparison, the superiority of the Australians is so marked.'[64] George Ernest Morrison was in agreement and used the stores as examples of what might be achieved if Australia took the China market more seriously:

> There seems to be a complete misconception in Australia of the importance of the China market. I enclose to you a picture of a new department store which has just been opened in Shanghai under the direction of Australian trained Chinese . . . This is only one of a number of these department stores.[65]

The Wing On Department Store was the second Chinese Australian enterprise to open on Nanjing Road, which was within the International Settlement. The managers had drawn on their Wing On business in Australia, as well as relatives in America and Australia, to accumulate enough capital to open their first store in Hong Kong in 1907.[66] Both stores employed hundreds of staff from the Gock brothers' ancestral village of Chuk Sau Yuen, as well as neighbouring villages in Guangdong.[67] These areas were among the first in Guangdong to install electricity and running water in village homes due to capital flowing in from the Wing On business. In China the advent of the department store coincided with the rapid expansion of Chinese capitalism, creating what John Wu has called a golden age (*huangjin shiqi*) of national industrialisation between 1910 and 1920. This era of economic opportunity for Chinese entrepreneurs, 'when the colonial powers were less occupied with their colonial footholds in Asia, was also the era of political revolution'.[68] The goals of the Republican revolution in China were linked: to rid China of imperialism, so blatantly symbolised by the treaty ports, and to make China into a strong and modern nation state.[69] Chinese Australians in Shanghai were to play a key role in the unfolding of these events.[70]

As members of this elite class of patriotic returned overseas Cantonese in Shanghai, Daisy and her siblings attended a Cantonese school for students of returned overseas Chinese but struggled as they could not speak Cantonese or Shanghainese. Even their names were lost in translation. As they had never been given Chinese names, the teacher wrote them each a new name on a piece of paper. But Daisy forgot hers, and the piece of paper was blown out of her hand on the way home.[71] 'Life at the Cantonese school was a nightmare for me,' Daisy wrote in a draft of her memoirs.

> All three of us [Kwok siblings], in spite of the difference in age, were put in the first grade to begin learning Chinese. I just couldn't pronounce the

words correctly. Every day I just cried and cried. Then we were put in the highest class for English . . . again I couldn't keep up. The reader was too difficult for me.[72]

The family became close to a Chinese girl from Jamaica who lived in the nearby Burlington Hotel. She recommended the girls attend the prestigious McTyeire School run by American missionaries. At McTyeire they no longer had any language difficulties, as the classes were all in English. Daisy would come to regret this turn of events:

> Neglecting our study of Chinese was a big mistake, one I have regretted all my life. I did not realize how much I was handicapped until I graduated from college. However, at the time Shanghai was a city ruled by the foreign imperialists. Everyone spoke English. It seemed more important to know English than Chinese. I remember attending a meeting of the Shanghai Chinese Women's Club, and was surprised to find the meeting was conducted in English. Other international Women's Clubs held meetings in their own language. In the big department stores attendants had to know English to get a job. Even some rickshaw coolies could speak a few words.[73]

Her need for Chinese still far in the future, Daisy was relieved by the move to McTyeire, where the famous Soong sisters were among her classmates, and where she took prominent roles in Shakespeare plays such as *The Taming of the Shrew*. A society such as the one she would encounter in 1960s China, where such things were shameful, bourgeois and dangerous, would have been beyond anyone's expectations during this period.

The Kwok family moved to a mansion on Lucerne Road on what was then the outskirts of the International Settlement. Set back from the street behind large wrought-iron gates and sitting on a long green lawn, the mansion had been built and designed by a Swiss architect who had kept his Chinese mistress hidden in one of the mansion's upper wings.[74] Inside, chandeliers lit up frescoes of Swiss chalet scenes complete with smiling Aryan children and cows grazing against Alpine mountains.[75] The decision to move to the area signalled Kwok Bew's intimacy with the Republican government, whose ministers occupied many of the adjacent mansions – the Finance Minister, T. V. Soong, ate at the Kwok home once a week.[76] George Kwok Bew's connection with KMT in Shanghai enabled his family to join other high social groups and clubs in Shanghai. The family home was once used for a public celebration when Dr Sun was elected as President again in 1919.[77]

Marina Mar, whose uncle William Liu helped to open the Sun Sun Department Store, a successor to Wing On, travelled to Shanghai as a child.[78] She remembered these days in the early 1930s as a 'wonderful' time filled with visits to luxury homes and recalled being instantly struck by 'the big mansions' and opulent lifestyle of Chinese Australian émigrés in the city.[79] Daisy recalled the garden of her house better than its furnishings; she often worked pruning flowers with her father, who had become a keen horticulturist during his days as a Sydney market gardener: 'He always wound little pieces of string into balls and placed them in drawers, something he started doing in his days as a market gardener.'[80]

George Kwok Bew was appointed head of the Central China Mint in the 1920s and security was heightened for the children, as the family's political connections and association with Wing On made them possible targets for kidnappings and ransom. The Kwok children rarely went out. Men were allowed more freedom of movement than women. Daisy's elder brothers, now in their late teens, were granted access to the 'Seventh Heaven Wing' of Wing On, where they threw lavish parties and entertained girlfriends and mistresses.[81] Daisy's father also left the house frequently, as he had taken a Chinese mistress and started a second family. Daisy remembered her father's mistress (whom she called Yi Tai Tai) coming to the house to see her mother. Daisy 'did not like her because she had taken away her father'.[82]

As the Kwok girls grew older, they were put under increasing pressure to act as visual and moral representations of the Wing On brand. Aware that they were on show, they attended parties frequented by American film stars such as Douglas Fairbanks, Sr, dressed in the latest fashions and were among the first women to learn to drive in Shanghai.[83] Daisy appeared in local plays, specialising in English-language versions of Chinese classics, and captained the North China women's tennis team.[84] When she visited the Wing On Department Store, her behaviour was closely scrutinised by patrons and management. Daisy remembers being admonished by her brother when she couldn't find what she needed in the store, as a crowd had gathered outside to watch her shop.[85] The sisters walked a fine line between embodying a Westernised consumer culture and not appearing to support European imperialism in China or dishonour Chinese traditions around femininity and feminine exposure. In 1929 Daisy's sister Elsie was criticised after winning the Miss Shanghai beauty pageant, organised by Chinese Australian Yinson Lee to raise money for his charity.[86] In order to win the contest, she had campaigned for votes, leading one journalist to criticise her 'Coney Island' salesmanship techniques: 'there is a thing such as shyness in Chinese womanhood'.[87] The fact that her winnings included a car or a trip to Hollywood attracted satire from those who implied that her motives were shallow and unpatriotic, especially considering China's large and controversial trade deficit with Europe and America, which had sparked anxieties over the loss of sovereignty implicit in the growing foreign dominance of the commercial economy.[88]

By 1928 Daisy was living in Peking, where she became engaged to Albert Suez, the son of a family friend. While Albert was studying in America, she stayed with his family. There she reconnected with a childhood friend, Suzanne Lu, whose father had once been the Chinese consul to Australia. Suzanne was studying at Peking's Yenching University and, upon hearing her advice, Daisy broke off her engagement to Albert and decided to join Suzanne at Yenching instead, where she graduated with a degree in psychology in 1933. Albert threatened to kill her and even followed her to a train station in Peking with a gun.[89] Daisy would marry another man – MIT graduate Y. H. Woo – in 1934.

Figure 1.4 Pearlie Kwok, photographed when she was a bridesmaid at the wedding of Madame Chiang Kai-shek, 1 December 1927.

Source: Private Collection of Bobby Fu.

Figure 1.5 Four daughters with their mother, *c.*1928. Edith (far left), Darling
(seated at front), Elsie (standing at back), Pearlie (seated on right) and
Daisy Kwok (far right).

Source: Private Collection of Bobby Fu.

If Chinese Australian women were considered too Western by Chinese
nationalists like Albert, Shanghai's white colonial elites considered them
too Chinese to sanction socially. In European clubs and hotels they were either
banned entry or forced to use the service elevators, as the main elevators were
reserved for Europeans.[90] In Catherine Ladds' words, 'the allegiances of Chinese
communities in the British empire were particularly suspect because of the strong
ties that they maintained with family and business networks in China'.[91] 'They
never become good British subjects in the sense of developing a loyalty to the
Empire or feeling a community of interest with the British commonwealth of
nations', surmised the British consul general in Shanghai in 1927.[92]

White Australians in the city were especially vigilant in their monitoring of these
racial lines.[93] The ANZAC Society, of which Rex Phillips was a member, blocked
Chinese Australians from becoming members or entering their club room, leading
to an outcry in the Chinese Australian newspaper *United China* in 1931. The
newspaper's editor, Vivian Yung Chow, responded by finding similarities between
Chinese Australians and British settler colonists. He wrote of Chinese Australians
as no different from white Australians (as 'brothers within the British Empire'),
describing the 'great part that the early Chinese pioneers played in the up building
of the Australian nation,' and the vital role played by Chinese Australians as
mediators between 'the world's oldest civilization and the youngest of the

nations'.[94] In 1925 Chinese Australian Yinson Lee wrote a similar editorial criticising the Shanghai Club for not allowing Chinese membership, or even Chinese visitors, and describing the restriction as 'race discrimination'.[95] Responding to Yinson Lee's protest, the Shanghai Club pointed to the segregated nature of Shanghai's social world more generally. After all, it argued, it was not as if Europeans were accepted into Chinese clubs either.[96]

These debates over inclusion and exclusion were played out in other ways in Chinese Australian families where 'Asian', 'Australian' and 'Eurasian' identities were deeply contested, leading to the obliteration or deliberate forgetting of certain kinds of Eurasian connections and a corresponding emphasis on 'pure' Chinese connections.[97] Paul Kwok grew up in the wider Chinese Australian Kwok clan in interwar Shanghai. Daisy Kwok was his aunt, and his father worked for the Wing On Department Store. In 1934 Wing On sent his father to Manchester to study textile chemistry so that he could better manage his own cotton mills in Shanghai. There he met his wife, Edith Spliid, through mutual friends and the couple became engaged, marrying in Hong Kong in 1937. Because he was marrying a 'foreigner', Paul's grandmother refused to attend the wedding. When the couple travelled to Shanghai with the Kwok family after the wedding, she insisted on leaving on a different boat so she would not be forced to travel with the interracial couple. Paul recalls that, although his mother was eventually accepted by the family, she endured long years of hardship and social isolation due to her status as a European woman in a Chinese family.

Social censure, of course, was just as bad, if not worse, in white Australian communities in Shanghai, where 'the rules of social intercourse were rigid'.[98] White Russians and Jews were regarded by most as second-class citizens; Eurasians were ostracised; 'one mixed with other westerners of the right class'.[99] Shame surrounded children of mixed-race marriages or Westerners who crossed the boundaries of 'ethnic separateness' to marry. When Rex Phillips' friend and fellow Australian Tom Vickers started a family with his White Russian wife, Rex and his wife Madge ended their friendship with him. Sympathy and attention focused especially on the imagined plight of the Vickers' children: 'They're certainly half castes alright. One is bad enough but she has three . . . Over in this bog one has to try and forget and forgive, but I'm afraid I couldn't in this case of course, you savee?'[100]

Such prejudices were not evenly spread across the white Australian community in Shanghai. Racial boundaries could be overlooked, especially when the need to build economic ties aligned Chinese elites with non-Chinese elites. V. G. Bowden, Australian Trade Commissioner in Shanghai from 1935 to 1941, socialised regularly with the Kwoks and noticed that, by 1936, mixed foreign and Chinese parties were increasingly common. Bowden used these occasions to maintain good links with the Chinese socially and professionally and saw the mixed-race Hsui Club as an ideal location for these activities. The club formed 'a pleasant meeting place for the best classes of foreigners and Chinese'.[101] Bowden had good reason to be grateful to Shanghai's Chinese Australians. His appointment as Trade Commissioner was the result of the Australian Goodwill Trade Mission, led by John Latham in 1934, which had been warmly received in the city by the heads

Figure 1.6 Paul Kwok's parents, Edward Tai Chiu Kwok and Edith Spliid, on their wedding day, Hong Kong, 14 October 1937.

Source: Personal collection of Paul Kwok.

of the Chinese Australian department stores. Declaring Shanghai 'a clearing house of immense importance in terms of trade' and an 'obvious place for a trade commissioner,' Latham had reported:

We had great pleasure in meeting a number of Australian-born Chinese who now hold leading positions in the commercial world of China. Their kindness and courtesy knew no bounds and they could not do enough for us. The largest retail trading concerns in Shanghai (as well as Hong Kong and Canton) are conducted by these men and are in fact developments of a most striking nature from the parent concerns in Sydney (Wing On and Co., and Wing Sang and Co.). These are the Sincere Company, the Sun Sun Company and Wing On and Co., embracing enterprises ranging from large and very efficient department stores to immense cotton spinning mills with huge turnovers. It was a very pleasant thing to receive so warm a welcome from those who, although Chinese by race, hold Australia in high affection.[102]

It was the Kwok and Ma families who had arranged business luncheons for Latham and the Goodwill Mission while he was in the city, leading him to comment that he received more help from Australian Chinese than from the British consul general.[103]

Such cross-racial solidarities were not in evidence in other Australian expatriate circles in China. Charles Lee, the first Chinese Australian diplomat appointed to the Australian mission in Chungking in the 1940s, was banned from diplomatic functions due to the Australian ambassador's belief that he was of 'inferior intelligence'.[104] Australia's mission deputy, Keith Waller, was conflicted about Lee's level of appointment, saying the British 'are quite willing to treat us on the basis of equality but they resent the idea of a Chinese being so treated'. He conceded there were 'many arguments in favour of getting away from the idea of the whites being a superior race' but 'you cannot take a low-class oriental and turn him into a high-class European'. He complained: 'The poor wretch does not speak English, let alone Chinese.'[105] While in Chungking, Lee became engaged to the daughter of Chiang Kai-shek's chief physician. The couple were advised not to marry, as, if they did, Lee would forfeit his certificate of naturalisation as Australian-born. According to David Sadleir, a former head of ASIO who worked with Lee in both Singapore and Manila, where Lee was a counsellor, he was 'treated with outrageous racism'. Sadleir attributes his own career success in Manila to Lee. Lee befriended the Chinese community there and had excellent networks. Other ambassadors were aware of this and held Lee in high regard. When the German ambassador asked to see Lee personally, the Australian ambassador told Lee: 'I wouldn't bother about that, Charles, he is far too smart for you.'[106]

In interwar Shanghai Chinese Australian and white Australian émigré groups managed the 'problem' of racial mixture and interracial encounter through what Nancy Green terms 'family governance'.[107] Confronting the unstable conceptions of their ethnicity and nationality became unavoidable, as race became the primary category of social analysis in Shanghai, governing employment opportunities and public space; the interwar period witnessed efforts to purify and redefine Eurasian identity and history in order to secure the position of Eurasians within this changing world. As Chinese Australian and white Australian émigrés attempted to define and discipline unruly Eurasian family relationships, this struggle became submerged within the complex divisions of class, education and occupation within the community. At particular moments interactions were clearly inscribed into their everyday lives – the language they spoke, the food they ate and how they ate it, and the clothes they wore.

In 1937, the year Japan invaded China, Chinese Australian Ann Chung Gon travelled from Tasmania to Shanghai to stay with the Kwok family in their Lucerne Road mansion. When Ann returned to Australia in December, she was interviewed by the *Examiner* newspaper.[108] Asked if she wore her 'native costume' in China or dressed in Western clothes, 'Miss Chung said "I had to dress in native costume otherwise I was mistaken for a Jap wherever I went".' She told the paper that 'seventy percent of the people mistook her for a Japanese when she was dressed in western clothes and she received very cool reception and even dangerous scowls from the coolies'.[109] As a Chinese Australian, Ann Chung Gon's position in China tracked back and forth between local class divisions, transnational family networks and geopolitical conflicts, while her racial status, she thought, was read through her choice of Western or Chinese clothing. Confronted while wearing Western dress by lower-class workers in the docks of Asian treaty ports, she felt herself the object of 'coolie' derision, and on the streets of Shanghai she felt these clothes aligned her with Japanese imperialism. In Chinese clothing, however, she believed her outsider status as Australian-born Chinese was clarified, or at least harder to read as 'foreign'.

In interwar Shanghai, white Australians and Chinese Australians were acutely aware of each other's quotidian social behaviour. While Rex Phillips liked to slot Australian-born Chinese into the familiar imperial racial hierarchies he remembered from Australia, men and women like George Kwok Bew and Daisy Kwok Bew were, in some ways, his social superiors in the city, enjoying a lifestyle uncomfortably similar to his own. We are 'your brothers in Empire', Yinson Lee had written. Being a member of the Australian-born Chinese community in early twentieth-century Shanghai seemed, in many ways, to be cemented by a collective class identity and common public and social spaces, rather than by any meaningful ethnic identity. This was especially the case for Chinese Australian women, whose bodies were anxiously puzzled over for clues as to their class position in competing political and imperial cultures.

As the experience of Australian-born Chinese shows, empire divided people as much as it united them. For the Kwok family in the 1930s, these divisions coalesced around the legality of their claims to British citizenship while living in Hong Kong and Shanghai. In the eyes of the Kwoks – carriers of British citizenship due to their Australian birth – these legal categories carried serious economic weight, for any change in their status curtailed their mobility within the British Empire and, therefore, their ability to operate their businesses. Most returned overseas Chinese in Chinese treaty ports were able to draw upon international family ties to assist them in moving between cultures to cross borders. However, the 'traversing of racial and imperial frontiers generated a counter impulse to delimit the type of people who were entitled to be British'.[110]

In China, the imperative to extend British authority over as many people as possible, the lack of a clearly defined returned overseas Chinese and Eurasian community, the fact that most overseas Chinese and Eurasians were born outside of British territory, and the relative autonomy of consuls led to a highly individualised approach to determining the status of Eurasians until the late 1920s.[111] Children born in the treaty ports could not claim British nationality automatically on the basis of place of birth, meaning that the power of deciding upon the subjecthood of Eurasians resided with the consuls. When Daisy's brother, Leon Kwok Bew, applied to have his Shanghai-born daughter registered as a British citizen in 1928, his applications were repeatedly rejected, despite the fact that his sons Victor and Gerald, born in Shanghai a few years earlier, were registered without difficulty. As Leon put it in a letter to the British consul general:

> It seems strange that after registering my sons you would hesitate to do likewise with my daughter. It is my desire to send her to Australia for education in later years and I would appreciate it if you would re-consider your decision. Several of my friends, who are British subjects, have informed me that their children born in Shanghai recently were registered by you without prejudice or objection.[112]

The consulate defended the decision on the basis that the Kwoks, despite being from Sydney, were of 'Chinese race', and because the 'children of British citizens of Chinese race born in China cannot be registered'. The consulate eventually changed its mind, however, on the basis that the Kwoks were Chinese from the Dominions and not from the Straights Settlements or Hong Kong, ruling that it was important to 'distinguish between the two'.[113] Leon was able to register his daughter as a British citizen in 1929.

Because Chinese Australians were people who occupied the margins of racial categories and lived on the edges of empire, their life trajectories starkly illuminate the ambiguities inherent in attempts to articulate a unified vision of imperial belonging. For one, their navigation of treaty port China exposed the entwined privileges and prejudices which characterised their lives in these places, as well as the disquiet felt by Anglo-Australians and British authorities towards the multi-national society that they had helped to create in the treaty ports. These were cities, in Catherine Ladds' words, 'in which the imperial loyalty of British subjects could be supplanted by cosmopolitan sensibilities'.[114]

By situating the multinational world of the China coast within broader concerns about Australia's future in Asia after the First World War, this chapter has sought to demonstrate how shifting understanding of the relationship between race and national belonging affected the mobility of people who fell between the boundaries of colonial racial categories and whose worlds spanned the South China Sea. The specific exigencies of British power on the China coast, the rise of Chinese nationalism, and Australia's own attempts to square racialist thinking with an economic drive into Asia collided with increasing barriers to migration across the empire world. As a result, many Chinese Australians faced continuing challenges in their quest to sustain their mobility between Australia and China. Most of those who survived the war with Japan fled China after 1949, where the new communist government embarked on an ambitious plan to erase racial ambiguity by assigning one of fifty-six ethnic categories to each individual.[115]

Emma Teng has argued that a narrative of prejudice has dominated discussion of Eurasian histories at the expense of recognising how the ability to cross between cultures also conferred privilege.[116] By examining the life of the Kwok family in

Shanghai up until 1949, we can follow the journeys of Chinese Australians around the world of empire in the early twentieth century. In doing so, I consider how these dual forces of privilege and prejudice impinged upon individual life trajectories. During an age of hostility towards Chinese migration, the adjuncts to a mixed identity, which could include integration into transimperial networks of friends and family, possession of a British passport and the ability to demonstrate Australian cultural traits, sometimes enabled Chinese Australians, such as Daisy Kwok and her family, to cross borders that were otherwise closed to Chinese migrants. However, the ability to access these privileges was constrained by gender, social class, perceived cultural habits, locality and shifting legal definitions of nationality.

Notes

1 Chen Danyan, *Shanghai Princess* (陈丹燕著，上海的金枝玉叶）(Taibei Shi: Erya chubanshe, 1999), 15; Chen Danyan, *Shanghai Princess: Her Survival with Pride and Dignity* (New York: Better Link Press, 2010).
2 George Ernest Morrison to W. A. Watt, Head of the Melbourne Chamber of Commerce, Peking, 17 September 1918, in Lo Hui-Min (ed.) *The Correspondence of George Ernest Morrison 1862–1920* (New York: Cambridge University Press, 1976).
3 Laura Madokoro, 'Surveying Hong Kong in the 1950s: Western "Humanitarianism" and the Problem of Chinese Refugees', *Modern Asian Studies* 49.2 (2015): 493.
4 Bernice Archer, *The Internment of Western Civilians under the Japanese 1941–1945* (London: Routledge, 2004), 54–56. For a first-hand account see: Hugh Collar, *Captive in Shanghai: A Story of Internment in World War II* (Hong Kong: Oxford University Press, 1990).
5 'Australian Internees – Shanghai – Lists of Internees [55 pp. including duplicate copies], 1945–1946', NAA A4144 228/1947; 'Australian Internees – Shanghai, 1945–1945', NAA A4144 228/1945. See also: Roger Zetter, 'Labelling Refugees: Forming and Transforming a Bureaucratic Identity', *Journal of Refugee Studies* 4.1 (1991): 36–62.
6 'Internees, Australians Abroad, Far East. Kennedy A.R. Mission to Internment Camp Shanghai, 1945–1945', NAA A1066 IC45/55/3/13; 'Internees Australian Abroad, Far East Kennedy A. R. Mission to Internment Camp, Shanghai 1945–1945', NAA A1066 IC45/55/3/13.
7 'Australian Internees – Shanghai – Lists of Internees [55 pp. including duplicate copies], 1945–1946', NAA A4144 228/1947; 'Australian Internees – Shanghai, 1945–1945', NAA A4144 228/1945.
8 At the end of the Second World War, displaced overseas Chinese defied easy categorisation and posed unique challenges. As Elaine Ho demonstrates, they were not only the product of forced migration and broadly unwanted as repatriates, but they were also a population that left nominally temporary overseas residences and returned to their ancestral homeland. See: Meredith Oyen, 'Forum Article. The Right of Return: Chinese Displaced Persons and the International Refugee Organization, 1947–56', *Modern Asian Studies*, 49.2 (2015): 549.
9 The Swiss consul general counted 594 Australians in total in his list. See: 'Australian Internees – Shanghai – Lists of Internees [55 pp. including duplicate copies] 1945–1946', NAA A4144 228/1947. I have not managed to find

statistics for the number of Chinese Australians residing in Shanghai in the first half of the twentieth century; however, we can track the sharp drop in the total Chinese Australian population in Australian data. For example, census figures record 32,700 Chinese residents in Australia in 1901 and just half that number in 1939 (30,000 to 15,000). The Great Depression contributed to a sharp drop in the early 1930s. Chinese Australians made up 14.1 per cent of the total population in 1931 and 2.09 per cent in 1936. See: 'Chinese in Australia', NAA A1/1906/7525.

10   Oyen, 'Forum Article', 546–571.

11   Margaret Allen makes this argument for Indian Australians. See: Margaret Allen, '"Innocents abroad" and "Prohibited immigrants": Australians in India and Indians in Australia 1890–1910', in Ann Curthoys and Marilyn Lake (eds.) *Connected World: History in Transnational Perspective* (Canberra: ANU ePress, 2005), 111–125. See also: Margaret Allen, 'The Australian Horse Trader's Winter in Calcutta 1930', *JOSA Journal of the Oriental Society of Australia* 39–40, part 1 (October 2008): 37–49; 'Shadow Letters and the "Karnana" Letter: Indians Negotiate the White Australia Policy, 1901–1921', *Life Writing* 8.2 (June 2011): 187–202; '"That's the Modern Girl": Missionary Women and Modernity in Calcutta, *c.*1907–*c.*1940', *Itinerario* 34.3 (2010): 83–96.

12   William Liu, 'Australia's Chinese Connection', 125th Anniversary of the Battle of Eureka Stockade: Fifth Annual Lalor Address on Community Relations, Commissioner for Community Relations, Canberra, 1979, 19–27.

13   Quoted in Michael Williams, 'Sojourn in Your Native Land', Master's Thesis, University of New England, 1998.

14   Emily Honig, 'Migrant Culture in Shanghai: In Search of a Subei Identity', in Frederic Wakeman, Jr. and Wen-hsin Yeh (eds.) *Shanghai Sojourners*, Chinese Research Monograph 40 (Berkeley: University of California Press, 1992), 239–266. According to Japanese scholar Sugihara Kaoru's estimates, over the entire period from 1869 to 1939 approximately 14.7 million people left China from the ports of Xiaomen, Shantou and Hong Kong, while a total of 11.6 million persons returned to China between 1873 and 1939.

15   From 1885 to 1935 Shanghai natives accounted for an average of only 19 per cent of the population of the entire International Concession and 26 per cent of the Chinese-owned parts of the city. Zou Yiren, *Jiu Shanghai renkou bianqian de yanjiu* (Research on Changes in the Population of Old Shanghai) (Shanghai: Shanghai renmin chubanshe, 1980), 112–113.

16   Angela Woollacott, *To Seek Her Fortune in London: Australian Women, Colonialism and Modernity* (London: Oxford University Press, 2001).

17   Mei-fen Kuo, *Making Chinese Australians: Urban Elites, Newspapers and the Formation of Chinese-Australian Identity, 1892–1912* (Melbourne: Monash University Press, 2013).

18   John Fitzgerald, 'Equality and the "Unequal Treaties": Chinese Émigrés and British Colonial Routes to Modernity', in Bryna Goodman and David S. Goodman (eds.) *Twentieth-Century Colonialism and China: Localities, the Everyday and the World* (London: Routledge, 2012), 180–196; Rodney Noonan, 'Grafton to Guangzhou: The Revolutionary Journey of Tse Tsan Tai', *Journal of Intercultural Studies* 27.1–2 (February–May 2006): 101–115.

19   Interview with Tess Johnston, Shanghai, November 2014.

20   By 1921 Eurasian-Chinese Australians made up over 15 per cent of the total Chinese Australian population nationwide. See: 'Chinese in Australia', NAA A1/1906/7525; 'Chinese Communities – Recording and Filing System and Number of Chinese in Australia', NAA A373/1/9774. This file shows that in 1944 there were 7,686 Chinese in Australia (587 women and 7,099 men).

21   Antonia Finnane, *Far from Where? Jewish Journeys from Shanghai to Australia* (Carlton: University of Melbourne Press, 1999), 37.

22   In its 1953 national census figures, the government claimed there were just over 11.7 million 'Overseas Chinese' worldwide, made up of ethnic Chinese, regardless of nationality, who lived outside the territorial border of the Chinese state. By the end of the same decade, there were said to be an almost equal number (approximately 11 million) of domestic Overseas Chinese, according to official sources. Part of this group was known as Returned Overseas Chinese (*guiguo huaqiao*) or *Guiqiao*. By 1960 there were up to 60,000 *Guiqiao* in China, following several major waves of return migration. See also: 宋钻友 著 (Song Zuanyou zhu), 广东人在上海 (年) (Guangdong ren zai Shanghai [1843– 1949]) (Shanghai: Shanghai renmin chubanshe, 2007).

23   V. Y. Chow, 'Anzac Society's Disservice to Australia', *United China*, December 1935, 25.

24   Evelyn Yin Lo, quoted in Mavis Gock Yen, 'Memories of Sydney's Chinatown', in Susan Hamilton and Renata Klein (eds.) *Australia for Women* (Sydney: Spinafex, 1994), 39–47.

25   Peter Thompson, *Shanghai Fury: Australian Heroes of Revolutionary China* (London: Random House, 2011).

26   John Fitzgerald, *Big White Lie: Chinese Australians in White Australia* (Sydney: University of NSW Press, 2006); Kuo, *Making Chinese Australians*; Paul Macgregor, 'Crossing between Cultures: A Watershed in Chinese–Australian Relations Came in 1949–50', *International Relations Quarterly Supplement – National Library of Australia News* (1994): 12–16.

27   Agniezska Sobocinska, 'Overturning the Point: Exploring Change in Australia– Asia Relations', *History Compass* 12.8 (2014): 642–650.

28   Email correspondence between the author and ex-Australian consul general to Shanghai Murray Mclean and consul staffer Evan Williams, 12 December 2014 and 1 February 2015.

29   'Chen Danyan and Her Shanghai Princess', China.org.cn, 8 September 2005. 陈丹燕著, 上海的金枝玉叶 (Taibei Shi: Erya chubanshe, 1999).

30   Chen, *Shanghai Princess*.

31   Kirsty Walker, 'Intimate Histories: Eurasian Family Histories in Colonial Penang', *Modern Asian Studies* 46.2 (2012): 303–329.

32   Ibid., 313. See also: Niall Green, 'The Hajj as Its Own Undoing: Infrastructure and Integration on the Muslim Journey to Mecca', *Past and Present* (February 2015): 224.

33   A key tenet of the White Australia Policy was the complete eradication of Asian populations in Australia. Thriving Chinese Australian communities in the interwar period put a lie to the claim that this aspect of the policy had been successful. In 1908 Attlee Hunt, a chief author of Australia's Immigration Restriction legislation, defended the policy to the Japanese consul general by arguing: 'What would be the consequences of that [an Asiatic man being allowed to live with his wife in Australia]? Immediately a family would spring up, there would be, say, four sons. When these reached manhood what would be their position? They would be British subjects born here, with all our rights. How are they to be treated? Are they compelled to take white wives or are we to permit them to introduce wives of their own blood from abroad and thus perpetuate the existence in Australia of a people whose presence is not desired?' Attlee Hunt to E. W. Foxall, Japanese consul general, Sydney, Melbourne, 8 December 1908, Attlee Hunt papers, NLA. My thanks to Michael Williams for bringing this reference to my attention.

34   Nancy Green, 'Forms of Comparison', in Deborah Cohen and Maura O'Connor (eds.) *Comparison and History: Europe in Cross-National Perspective* (New York:

Routledge, 2004), 41–57. See also: Philippa Levine, 'Is Comparative History Possible?', *History and Theory* 53 (October 2014): 331–347.

35   Chow, 'Anzac Society's Disservice to Australia', 25.

36   Daisy Kwok's birth certificate, NSW Births Deaths and Marriages. My thanks to Kate Bagnall for bringing this certificate to my attention.

37   Email correspondence between Terence Fu and Maunie Kwok, 15 October 1998. My thanks to Paul and Maunie Kwok for kindly sharing this correspondence with me.

38   *Zhongshan ren zai aozhou* (Zhongshan People in Australia), *Zhongshan wenzhi* (Records of Zhongshan) No. 24 (Guangzhou: Zhengxie guangdongsheng zhongshanshi weiyuanhui wenshi weihuanhui, 1992), 84–90 and 198–219.

39   'Materials Relating to Daisy Kwok', Tess Johnston papers, HI, 2015C32, Box 17, Folder 5.

40   Ibid.

41   Robert Norton, *The History of Wing On*, 28. My thanks to Paul and Maunie Kwok for lending me this pamphlet.

42   Kuo, *Making Chinese Australians*, 18.

43   Daisy's memoirs as quoted in Chen, *Shanghai Princess*, 8–13.

44   Chen, *Shanghai Princess*, 21.

45   'Eulogy for Mavis Gock Yen.' My thanks to Richard and Siaomen Horsburgh for kindly sharing this with me.

46   Gock family immigration files. See: 'George Bew [2 photographs attached], Leon Bew [2 photographs attached], Pearl Bew [2 photographs attached], Percy Bew [2 photographs attached], Daisy Alma Bew [2 photographs attached], George Noel Bew [2 photographs attached], Walter Bew [2 photographs attached], Elsie Bew [2 photographs attached], Edith Bew [2 photographs and birth certificate attached], Darling Bew [2 photographs and birth certificate attached] [Box 36]', NAA SP244/2, N1950/2/3885.

47   Chen, *Shanghai Princess*, 15.

48   Marilyn Lake, 'Chinese Colonists Assert Their Common Human Rights: Cosmopolitanism as Subject and Method in History', *Journal of World History* 21.3 (September 2010): 375–392.

49   Kuo, *Making Chinese Australians*, 127.

50   Ibid.

51   Michael Williams, 'Brief Sojourn in Your Native Land: Sydney's Huaqiao and Their Links with South China during the First Half of the Twentieth Century', MLitt Thesis, University of New England, 1998.

52   Fitzgerald, 'Equality and the "Unequal Treaties"', 181.

53   'Feng-Kwok Bew Wedding', *North China Herald*, 17 April 1920.

54   Papers of Rex, Clarence and Madge Phillips, 1924–1946, Manuscripts Collection, NLA, MS 9942.

55   'The Eastern and Australian Steamship Co Ltd, Tourist Guides: China, Japan, Islands and Ports en Route to Australia and Tasmania', *c.*1928, SFP, CoSA, CRS 188 Box 480–497, 'Shipping' Folder 489.

56   Recent work by Niall Green has drawn attention to the complex itineraries of hajj pilgrims in the age of steam. See: Green, 'The Hajj as Its Own Undoing', 204.

57   Lachlan Strahan, *Australia's China: Changing Perceptions from the 1930s to the 1990s* (Cambridge and New York: Cambridge University Press, 1996), 98.

58   Ibid., 104.

59   Colonel Thomas in Hong Kong, 'Colony Impressed with Significant Statement: Key to Far East: From Our Own Correspondent', *North China Herald*, 7 February 1934, 208.

60 Strahan, *Australia's China*, 104. See also: Memo 26 November 1947, NAA A1068/1 IC/47/5/2/5/1.
61 Quoted in Strahan, *Australia's China*, 105.
62 Ibid., 109.
63 'To Shanghai', Daisy Kwok personal writings, 'Materials Relating to Daisy Kwok'.
64 'China in Revolution' (Broadcast Lectures), *United China* 1.11 (October 1932): 454–456.
65 Morrison to Watt, 17 September 1918.
66 Fitzgerald, *Big White Lie*, 197.
67 Ibid., 199.
68 Kerrie L. MacPherson, *Asian Department Stores* (Richmond, Surrey: Curzon, 1998), 76.
69 Ibid., 76.
70 Song Zuanyou, *Cantonese Peoples in Shanghai* (宋钻友, 广东人在上海 (上海: 上海人民出版社, 2007) (Guangdong ren zai Shanghai).
71 Chen, *Shanghai Princess*, 30.
72 Daisy Kwok draft memoir, 'Materials Relating to Daisy Kwok'.
73 Ibid.
74 Tess Johnston and Deke Erh, *A Last Look: Western Architecture in Old Shanghai* (Hong Kong: Old China Hand Press, 1993), 20–21.
75 Interview with Tess Johnston, Shanghai, 25 October 2014.
76 Ibid.
77 I am grateful to Mei-fen Kuo for this information.
78 Fitzgerald, *Big White Lie*, 89. See also: Robert Bickers, 'Shanghailanders: The Formation and Identity of the British Settler Community in Shanghai', *Past and Present* 159 (May 1998): 161–211.
79 Fitzgerald, *Big White Lie*, 111.
80 Chen, *Shanghai Princess*, 33.
81 Email correspondence with Tess Johnston, 8 January 2014. Email communication with Paul Gock, 14 June 2015.
82 Tess Johnston interview; Chen, *Shanghai Princess*, 76.
83 'Over the Tea Cup: Relaxation and "Teeth-Ache": Douglas Fairbanks to Tea: Hearts and Cupid', *North China Herald*, 7 February 1931.
84 'Lady Precious Stream', Shanghai's Presentation at Carlton Theatre, *North China Herald*, 3 July 1935.
85 'Materials Relating to Daisy Kwok'.
86 'A Hard Task for Judicial Pars, Popularity Contest in Court: Judge's Advice to Settle', *North China Herald*, 23 November 1929.
87 Ibid.
88 Karl Gerth, *China Made: Consumer Culture and the Creation of the Nation* (Cambridge, MA: Harvard University Press, 2003).
89 'Materials Relating to Daisy Kwok'.
90 Tess Johnston interview.
91 For an overview of Chinese communities in Southeast Asia, and the ties to China that many of these migrants retained, see: Phillip A. Kuhn, *Chinese Among Others: Emigration in Modern Times* (New York: Rowman & Littlefield, 2008), 153–196.
92 TNA, FO 671/463, letter no. 115, J. F. Brenan, Shanghai, to Sir Miles Lampson, British minister to China, 4 July 1927.
93 Mrinalini Sinha, 'Britishness, Clubbability, and the Colonial Public Sphere: The Genealogy of an Imperial Institution in Colonial India', *Journal of British Studies* 40.4 'Special Issue: At Home in the British Empire' (October 2001): 489–521.

94 Chow, 'Anzac Society's Disservice to Australia', 25.
95 *North China Herald*, 8 August 1925; 'Why Are Returned Students Anti-foreign?', *North China Herald*, 4 April 1925. See also: Mei-fen Kuo: 'Everyday Life Approaches and Changing Perspectives in Diaspora Philanthropy: The Stories of Joe Tong and William Yinson Lee', in *Conference Proceedings: International Symposium on International Migration and Qiaoxiang Studies, Wu Yi University, Jiangmen, China, December 11–14 2014* (Wuyi University: Guangdong Qiaoxiang Cultural Research Center), 346–377.
96 Kuo, 'Everyday Life Approaches', 371.
97 Walker, 'Intimate Histories', 252.
98 Strahan, *Australia's China*, 104.
99 Ibid., 104.
100 Papers of Rex, Clarence and Madge Phillips, MS 9942.
101 Strahan, *Australia's China*, 105.
102 'Goodwill Trade Mission Report', NAA A981 FAR 5 PART 16, 75.
103 Ibid., 79.
104 'Charles Que Fong Lee, a Diplomat Who Overcame Racist Foes', *The Australian*, 9 July 2011.
105 Ibid.
106 Conversation with David Sadleir, 20 January 2016, Canberra.
107 Nancy Green, 'Forms of Comparison'.
108 'My Native Land: A Visit to China by a Tasmanian Born Chinese Girl, Miss Ann Chung Gon Interview', *The Examiner*, 22 December 1937, 7.
109 Ibid.
110 Catherine Ladds, 'Eurasians in Treaty-Port China: Journeys across Racial and Imperial Frontiers', unpublished chapter. I am grateful to the author for sharing her work with me prior to publication.
111 Ibid.
112 Leon Bew (known as Leon O. Kwok) to consulate general, Shanghai, 20 February 1928, 'The Oriental Trading Co., Importers and Exporters, Commonwealth Agents, Shanghai'. Leon On Bew (or Kwok) Registration of Children from Local in China', British Foreign Office Archives, 'British Subjects of Chinese Origin', C/8, 1923–32, FO 671/460, 3125/228/8. My thanks to Catherine Ladds for the reference.
113 'Leon Bew Application to Register Daughter's Birth, Leon On Bew (or Kwok) Registration of Children from Local in China', British Foreign Office Archives, 'British Subjects of Chinese Origin'.
114 Ladds, 'Eurasians in Treaty-Port China'.
115 T. S. Mullaney, *Coming to Terms with the Nation: Ethnic Classification in Modern China* (Berkeley: University of California Press, 2011).
116 E. J. Teng, *Eurasian: Mixed Identities in the United States, China, and Hong Kong, 1842–1943* (Berkeley: University of California Press, 2013), 9–10.

2   The Kwok Family After Liberation

*Certainly no one can say Australia is an imperialist country. No, most people
... think it's still a British colony where the people are oppressed.*[1]

Nien Cheng, *Life and Death in Shanghai*

Returned overseas Chinese are a forgotten legacy of China's treaty ports.[2] Between 1911 and the founding of the People's Republic of China in 1949, these returnees were a constitutive part of the communities born out of contact between China and the West in coastal enclaves such as Shanghai; Chinese Australians were especially influential in commercial circles. In the new society created after 1949, however, connections to the reviled imperialist past were dangerous, especially those that ran as deep as blood ties. People who had once asserted a Westernised identity now strove to become Chinese. Western connections and Australian ancestors, whose existence had once been exhibited as proof of entitlement to foreign passports and extraterritorial protection, were now quietly and deliberately forgotten.[3]

As Maoist China withdrew from the outside world, overseas Chinese elites that had previously drawn upon multinational affiliations and adeptness at cultural crossing in order to make international journeys were either forced to leave or immobilised.[4] Businesses were slowly taken over by communist forces and eventually nationalised; property was confiscated and family histories interrogated for evidence of a now-tainted connection to the West. For the Kwok family, 1949 spelled the end of their sprawling financial networks, as it was no longer possible to move people and goods across the mainland border.[5] The majority of the family retreated to Hong Kong, Singapore or the United States, where they remained throughout the Maoist period. It was only Daisy and her sister Pearlie who chose to stay in Shanghai.

Daisy's father, George Kwok Bew, would not live to see the fall of the Republican regime or the arrival of a communist government in 1949; he died suddenly of a stroke in 1932, leaving Daisy and her siblings to manage his vast estate. Obituaries celebrated a man who 'was much esteemed by all communities in Shanghai' and whose 'career spoke eloquently of the possession of unusual gifts which won success in two widely different centres of commercial activity'.[6] We know less about Darling Bew's death but she is believed to have passed away in the 1940s.

Some years earlier, Daisy's friend Mavis Gock Ming had also lost a parent. Her mother Mabel, 'the centre of the children's universe', had died of complications from smallpox in 1926, one year after the family had arrived in Shanghai from Sydney.[7] Mavis's father worked seven days a week for Wing On, so chose to remarry quickly in order to have help looking after his children. At fifty-two he married a sixteen- or seventeen-year-old Chinese woman, who was the same age as his eldest son.[8] The legacies of their parents' choices – to live across cultures and between countries – would shadow Daisy and Mavis in ways neither set of parents could have anticipated.

The fragile world of Chinese Australians in Shanghai began to collapse when the Japanese attacked Pearl Harbor and occupied the foreign concessions in China in December 1941. The struggle for the foreign concessions was a non-event; the last British troops had been withdrawn in August 1940 to bolster troops on the European fronts. The invasion of Hong Kong by the Japanese meant that remittances could no longer be sent through stores and agents based there. This drastically reduced the flow of money to the villages of overseas Chinese.[9] After the invasion, many Australian-born Chinese left Shanghai and returned to Australia. Evelyn Yin Lo remembered arriving in Sydney with 'lots of dresses, Shanghai style', which she wore in the streets of Sydney, ignoring the children who 'ran behind me poking their fingers saying I was wearing a dressing gown'.[10] Daisy Kwok spent part of the war in Hong Kong, while Mavis Gock Ming returned to Sydney. Most of their siblings and friends moved their families and belongings to Hong Kong, Australia or America. In the late 1930s and early 1940s, respectively, Mabel and Daisy both returned to China, a decision that would change their lives and see them cut off from their family members for nearly forty years.

After liberation 1950s–1960s

In 1949, after a protracted civil war (1945–1949) with its Nationalist rivals, the Chinese Communist Party (CCP) took control of the country. Mao Zedong announced the founding of a new nation, the People's Republic of China (PRC). Within years of establishing a national government, the CCP banned emigration and imposed strict entry/exit controls on the movement of people and capital, while the US-led international embargo against China quickly curtailed external trade with countries, such as Australia, outside the Soviet Bloc; the *huaqiao* era of unbounded movement had come to an end.[11] Pearlie Kwok, Daisy's elder sister, attempted to leave China and return to Australia between 1949 and 1950 but discovered that her passport was not recognised by the Department of Immigration, as there were doubts about its legality. Pearlie had left Australia when she was a teenager and, although her handprints were still on file, the department argued that the age gap was now too wide to match her current prints with those taken in 1917.[12]

Soon after 1949 the Wing On company became a joint state-owned enterprise and the remaining Kwok family left for the United States or Hong Kong, while

Figure 2.1 Chinese Australian Arthur Janne in uniform in Shanghai during the war with Japan.

Source: Private Collection of Brad Powe.

Note: After twenty years of education in Sydney, his accent was so bad that the locals thought – given his appearance – that he must be Japanese. He signed up to the militia to avoid the abuse he often received on the streets. On the back of the photograph he wrote: 'I'd grown or rather got thinner when this snap was taken. Taken about a month after the war started in Shanghai. Hope to recover what I lost in Hong Kong. I put in some strenuous time in that uniform.'

the department store continued to flourish. But Daisy Kwok decided to stay: she was running a scientific instruments company with her husband Woo Yu-Hsiang (or YH as she called him) – a graduate of MIT – and it was only just beginning to make money: 'We didn't have anything outside. Where would we go?'[13] In fact, her husband – whose own business career, he felt, had always been overshadowed by his wife's connection to Wing On – was revelling in the most successful professional period of the couple's lives. Much of this success was due to Daisy. As she recalled:

> YH was never good at making money. He was too fond of gambling. We hardly made ends meet until finally I was able to put on a good show. At one time I worked with the Chinese Medical Association, getting advertisements for their publications.[14]

In 1945, after the Japanese surrender, YH was put in charge of managing German property in Shanghai.[15] His cousin, S. Y. Liu, the Minister of Finance, arranged for YH to be given the job. He befriended German merchants and, after these merchants returned to Germany, they continued to trade with him – hence the success of the couple's scientific trading company. Later the firm merged into the government-owned Shanghai Machinery Import and Export Company.[16]

Daisy and YH lived in comfortable circumstances, relieved that the war was over, and they 'shared a widespread conviction that the 1950s would be China's golden age'.[17] While members of YH's family were leaving China as well, he told Daisy: 'When the Japanese were here, the people of Shanghai still lived a good life. There is nothing to fear from the Communists.'[18] The Woo family even kept their servants; the communists forbade them to discharge their domestic staff lest they aggravate the unemployment problem. Daisy went to Hong Kong for a brief period at this time but returned because she disliked the place and her husband needed her to assist in his professional affairs. Daisy's strategy for her family's survival does not fit neatly into existing explanations for Chinese capitalists' decisions to stay or return to China during the communist revolution of 1949. Typically, this decision making has been couched in nationalistic terms: 'I'll not stay abroad as a white Chinese [*bai Hua*, referring to Chinese at the time who were comparable to White Russian exiles from the Russian Revolution]', wrote Liu Hongsheng in the early 1950s.[19] As shown here, Daisy's motivations for returning from Hong Kong were complex and related more to the dynamics of her relationship than to geopolitical concerns. Mavis Gock Ming also stayed in China. By 1957 she was living in Peking and employed as an English language translator for Radio Peking. Since the late 1930s, she had been working with left-wing foreigners such as Rewi Alley to promote socialist agricultural ideas in China, setting up communes and training farmers.[20]

Outside China, scholars have explained Chinese capitalists' decisions to stay or leave the country in 1949 by shifting attention from their nationalism to their transnationalism. In *Emigrant Entrepreneurs*, Siu-Lun Wong has analysed the complex motivations driving Chinese industrialists to leave their cotton mills in Shanghai and move to Hong Kong during 1949, and has noted that 'it was not uncommon for the members of one family to go their separate ways',[21] with one or more staying in China while the others went abroad.

The fate of some of Daisy's friends and relatives who had returned to Australia from Shanghai seemed to confirm for her that she had, indeed, made the right decision to stay there. Evelyn Yin Lo, who arrived 'sad and homesick' in Sydney from Shanghai during the Pacific War, was quarantined for one month upon arrival, due to smallpox scares. She and her husband – an ex-diplomat – experienced a sharp drop in their standard of living. They had abandoned their assets in China and money was a problem. Unable to cook or afford a servant, Evelyn was confronted with domestic tasks that she had never been taught to do:

> I remember my late husband – he wanted me to cook a chicken – a live one. Here, they killed the chicken. I couldn't do it – I didn't know how. I opened the kitchen door a bit and I found the chicken flying around the kitchen, caught it wrapped in newspaper garbage. I asked a friend – how do you cook – how do you cook this?

She asked her Scottish neighbour for help with the laundry:

> She said to me 'and now I know you don't know how to work.' Now I think
> it's a great joke to me – but at the time I didn't. Why didn't I know? Why
> didn't I learn? Why didn't we HAVE to learn? . . . We ate a lot of bread.[22]

Chinese Australian families became increasingly worried about the well-being
of their relatives, as rumours of famine circulated outside of China. When Daphne
Lowe travelled, with great difficulty, from Australia to her family village outside
Guangzhou in 1958, she 'remembered that she had a red woollen coat and it
was a rare sight in the village, the children in the village actually followed her
around. They thought that all overseas Chinese were rich.'[23]

In Shanghai in the late 1950s Daisy too was experiencing a stark shift in her
economic fortunes. Food was scarce due to the devastating results of agricultural
collectivisations during the Great Leap Forward. The political reverberations of
these famines culminated in the anti-Rightist campaigns of 1957, which targeted
'capitalists', especially those with Western connections, and anyone against
collectivisation. At the time, YH was working as one of the heads of the instruments
company. Unwisely, given the shifting political climate, he continued to correspond
with German firms. Daisy was at a training camp 'where the capitalists of the
foreign trade corporations were sent to have their brains washed', when she was
told she should immediately return home as her husband had been arrested.[24]

When YH was called for interrogation in 1958, he went off, against Daisy's
advice, dressed in his finest silk gown and driving his own car.[25] He was arrested and
sent to Tialanqiao political prison for speaking out against government policy
and for his increasingly problematic friendships with foreigners. He stood accused
of defrauding the state of $64,000, a crime he would be cleared of posthumously
in the 1980s. After he was arrested, Daisy was ordered to repay the money and all
their property was confiscated, including her jewellery and clothing, wedding dress
and veil, and numerous photo albums. As Daisy wrote in her memoirs:

> They also took away all our cutlery. So I went to the Seventh Heaven
> Building [an extension of the Wing On Department Store] to the apartment-
> homes of the Kwok family upstairs who had already left Shanghai, and helped
> ourselves to what we needed.[26]

Daisy would not see her husband again; he died in prison three years later and
she was called to identify his body. The night he was arrested she was called to go
and pick up the by now very run-down car he had left at his offices. Most of his
colleagues had stopped driving, as it was now considered a politically unwise
pursuit, redolent of pre-liberation days. In drafts of her memoirs, Daisy recalled
picking it up: 'As I drove home in this car, which never should have been driven,
I thought YH must have known it was already un-drivable, and he was hoping
for an accident.'[27] For three years she sent him clean clothes each week but was
never allowed to see him: 'I used to mark every day on the calendar when my

husband was arrested on March 15th 1958. But after three months I gave up, forever wondering what the outcome would be.'[28] Then, one night a prison warden called and told her to come and claim her husband's body.[29]

The 1960s–1970s

In the 1960s returned overseas Chinese were an especially conspicuous target during political campaigns. Many were charged with being a fifth column for the spread of capitalism in China.[30] The new reality arrived at Daisy's doorstep in 1964, when Red Guards from her workplace marched into her home beating drums and shouting slogans. They took away most of her remaining belongings or sealed them into another room. Daisy told her maid that she could no longer afford to house and keep her, but the maid refused to leave, saying that she needed a 300 yuan severance fee for the fifteen years she had worked for Daisy, who subsequently sold her son's camera to cover the amount. They only received 278 yuan for the camera and so, to make up the balance, offered the maid a portable radio. The maid signed a receipt, knowing the radio was worth more than the balance.[31] By this stage Daisy's daughter was living in Beijing, training to be a ballet dancer, and had very little contact with her mother.

The Red Guards then notified Daisy that she would have to vacate her home. Along with her son, she was driven to the 'slums at Dingxi Road, into a small room

Figure 2.2 Pearl Fu (née Kwok), Daisy's sister, Bobby Fu, Daisy's grand-nephew, and Daisy Woo (née Kwok) in Shanghai in 1965.

Source: Private Collection of Bobby Fu.

at the turn of the stairs, just above the kitchen (Ting Zi Jian, as Shanghai people call it)'. There were no modern facilities, and she used to carry water to and from her room in a basin. After work she would go past a small restaurant to buy noodles, only to discover that she could barely afford two ounces of boiled noodles, which cost eight cents.[32] The maid, Jung Hua, decided that she would take over Daisy's old house as her own and did not move with the family.

Weeks after Daisy had settled in her one-room home, a stranger came up the stairs yelling her name. It was the maid's son, who accused Daisy of mistreating his mother and 'moving out without leaving her a cent'. He had come to collect the money Daisy owed his mother and threatened to bring the police with him if she didn't pay. Luckily, Daisy still had the receipt from Jing Hua proving the payment of a severance fee. She showed it to the son, who replied that 'she swore you never gave her a cent'. He departed, having accepted the proof of the receipt.[33]

The so-called 'Four Clean-Up Movement' also took place in 1964. Due to her background as a capitalist, Daisy was made the target of this movement at her workplace at the time, the Foreign Trade Spare Time College, where she had been teaching. A working group came from Beijing to conduct the movement and, knowing little about Daisy personally, focused instead on YH: 'they held my husband's wrong-doings against me. They said "The good man has died, but you were the brains behind his crimes and you have survived."' Each of Daisy's colleagues took turns to speak out against her: 'At first, I tried to defend myself by explaining why I had done certain things, but the more I explained the worse my crimes became. In the end I gave up, accepted the accusations, admitted my wrong doings.'[34]

To assist in the agricultural effort and to 'reform her capitalist mindset through labor', Daisy was ordered to begin work on a farm in the Jiangwan district, northeast of Shanghai, where she would be in charge of feeding the pigs.[35] She also cleaned toilets and dug pits for human waste. On the farm Daisy's inability to speak adequate Chinese led to her nickname of 'that old foreign woman'.[36] She was also sent to Qingpu County where she dug fishponds.[37] Daisy remembered these years as the most difficult time: 'We worked until 10pm but had to be back at the farm next morning at 7am. I did not get much sleep during those days and often fell asleep hanging onto a strap on the bus.'[38] Most of her salary went to paying YH's debt and the family was in need of money; for ten years, from the mid-1960s to 1970s, there was only twenty yuan to take care of her and her son. At that time her son was at university and the cost of attending was fifteen yuan. Daisy had to spend another three yuan for a bus pass, leaving only two yuan for a monthly allowance.[39]

Daisy wrote to her relatives abroad but only one responded – her brother Wally, who sent $8,000 as repayment on a loan she had once given him;[40] Daisy would not receive this money until the late 1970s, when some of the goods and money confiscated by the Red Guards were slowly returned. She was later separated from her son and sent to Chongming Island outside of Shanghai, where she peeled frozen cabbages in a factory. One assignment was to peel the outer layer off white cabbages that came from the north. They were to be exported to Hong Kong and the frozen leaves had to be removed before they were packed again: 'My fingers would be frozen stiff by the time I finished the day's work. That caused the arthritis I suffer from now. My fingers are disfigured and I can't grasp things tightly.'[41] 'You know, she really suffered a great deal', Daisy's friend Tess Johnston recounted. 'She was never imprisoned but was often segregated . . . So she had a pretty hard time of it.'[42]

After 1949 media coverage of communist China in the US and Australia, warning of 'Mass Red Killings in China' and 'Red Ransom Plots', in which overseas Chinese were imprisoned and forced to write to their families in the West for money, played into the worst fears of separated families.[43] Many were suspicious of letters coming out of China and purportedly written by their relatives. While Cold War coverage of China in Australia was undoubtedly coloured by unhelpful and anti-communist editorialising, Chinese Australian families had reason to be sceptical. Since the early 1950s the communist government had been running a quiet propaganda campaign, encouraging and sometimes forcing those with family overseas to write asking for remittances to be reinstated, in order to assist in boosting the PRC's economy.[44] Such ransom letters typically began with family members describing illness, poverty and other non-political forms of privation and ended with an urgent plea for assistance. In some instances, the letters were so distressing that their recipients were reportedly driven to suicide.[45] The Kwok family diaspora would certainly have been aware of these occurrences. For Daisy Kwok, this politicisation of that most intimate of transnational family rituals – letter writing – meant her pleas for assistance from family members overseas were usually met with silence.

There was no help to be had from the Australian government either. In the immediate period after the Second World War the Australian government, through its consulate in Chongqing, had assisted in the repatriation of white Australians from China, but no Australian-born Chinese were given assistance.[46] The consulate closed in 1951 and Australian-born Chinese with separated families were viewed as a possible fifth column for Communism in the West.[47] The Australian consulate in Chongqing had closed after the Australian government's decision not to recognise the PRC; its powers were curtailed and the consulate shut down.[48] When the PRC was founded in 1949, Australia retained diplomatic relations with the previous regime, which had established itself in Taiwan. It would be another twenty-three years before Australian prime minister Gough Whitlam would re-establish diplomatic relations, by signing the joint communiqué of 17 December 1972.

These views were echoed in Australian newspapers, starting in the early 1950s. The *Daily Mercury* warned readers that millions of Chinese abroad may turn out to be the 'Herrenvolk' of the Far East: 'That is, a strong China might try to exploit their presence in areas marked out for expansion.'[49] Meanwhile, the *Morning Bulletin*, in an article entitled 'Who Are the Overseas Chinese?', told its readers in 1954 that:

The struggle for Asia is made up of many little struggles and one of them is the fight for the favour of the overseas Chinese. It's a vague, hard to understand fight, and its outcome could decide the [communist] issue.[50]

If Australians conflated individual overseas Chinese lives with the wider tensions of the Cold War world, so too did Chinese communists in their encounters with Australian-born Chinese. In her memoir *Life and Death in Shanghai*, Nien Cheng remembers fearing for her daughter's safety during a Shanghai political campaign in the early 1960s and hoping that her Australian birth would protect her from criticisms over her capitalist background. 'Wasn't it lucky I was born in Australia rather than the United States or Britain?' her daughter told her in the early months of the Cultural Revolution:

> Certainly no one can say Australia is an imperialist country . . . most people . . . think it's still a British colony where the people are oppressed. They don't know that Australians are really British and only the kangaroos are natives.[51]

But by the time Nien Cheng was arrested after her daughter was killed by Red Guards in 1967, a different view was propagated among the revolutionaries, who interrogated her about her years in Australia: 'They thought Australia and the United States were one and the same place.'[52]

During the Cultural Revolution all domestic overseas Chinese, because of their historically rooted and continuing close economic, social and personal ties abroad, were an especially conspicuous target.[53] Many were denounced and at times persecuted as 'enemies of the people' and 'foreign spies' (*li tong wai guo*); sometimes they were attacked simply for wearing Western clothing and sporting Western hairstyles.[54] Daisy's sister Pearlie was once beaten so badly by a Red Guard that she had to be hospitalised.[55] Now living in Beijing, Mavis Gock Ming – Mavis Gock Yen since her marriage to a communist official – was imprisoned for her foreign connections and later sent to the countryside for re-education. She had considered fleeing China in 1957 – her daughter, Siaomen, recounts finding a 1957 Qantas flight schedule in her possessions – but had decided to stay.[56]

In the early years of the Cultural Revolution, numerous political meetings were organised to denounce overseas Chinese. By then in her sixties, Daisy's stories echo the experiences of others from her class in this period. As she wrote in her memoirs:

> Once they held a big meeting with over a hundred people present to accuse me of my crimes. I sat in front facing the group while different people got up to talk. The things they accused me of were so fantastic that I began enjoying listening to them.[57]

Because Daisy and her sister Pearlie were the last members of the Kwok family remaining in China, they bore the brunt of public anger against the Wing On Company as a lingering symbol of Westernised capitalism. At another meeting, a colleague said that, before 1949, whenever Daisy went shopping at the Wing On Department Store, she would sit on a sofa with a cup of tea in one hand and a cigarette in the other. Meanwhile, the sales girls paraded before her, holding up new stock. If she nodded, they would wrap up whatever she wanted. She would then jump into her new American car and leave.[58] Daisy wrote that such behaviour would have been impossible: 'I would have been swept out of my family long ago.'[59] 'Daisy said she rather enjoyed the denunciations made by her servants and "friends"', wrote Tess Johnston years later: 'All were so totally false or so wildly exaggerated that she was fascinated to hear all the lurid things she was supposed to have done.'[60]

Speaking English, once a mark of prestige, was now dangerous. One day, over lunch at the factory, Daisy spoke to another member of the 'capitalist class' in English. Asked what she intended to do during the break, Daisy said she wanted to go to the Park Hotel to buy bread. Then she added: 'You know the bread they make now is better than before Liberation in 1949.' After the break the teachers were unexpectedly told to wait in a small room downstairs. A roomful of people was waiting for them. The worker in charge asked all those who knew English to stand up in front and Daisy did so. She noticed that one of the workers who had shared a table with them at lunch was also present. He fetched the two other teachers who were at the same table to the front. He came forward and told Daisy to kneel down and told her to report what she had said while upstairs. Daisy told them in Chinese. He accused her of lying:

> 'I understand English,' he said, 'didn't you say the word "Park"'? You intended going to the park at lunchtime. Who were you going to meet there? And for what?' I told him I was going to the Park Hotel, not the park, 'Oh yes,' he said, 'you claimed that the bread after liberation was no good. Do you deny that you mentioned the park and bread?' That shows how things could be twisted. After a few more taps on the head with the broom the meeting was adjourned.[61]

Teaching English 1980s–1990s

By the late 1970s, the thawing of relations between China and the United States, and the end of the Cultural Revolution, gave way to a new period in China's relations with the wider world. Embassies and consulates slowly reopened and, along with the renewal of diplomatic ties, the importation of scientific and technical materials in the English language created a demand for English teachers.[62] Returned overseas Chinese like Daisy and Mavis found their English skills in demand once again. Nien Cheng remembered that English teachers were so highly sought after in the early 1980s that she was able to use her own language skills to barter on the black market: English lessons for medical care. Daisy attracted a dedicated circle of students, and it was perhaps her desire to practise and polish her own spoken English that led her to socialise frequently in foreign diplomatic circles.

Tess Johnston met Daisy at this time (they encountered each other at a party at the Australian consulate) and visited her small apartment in the French Concession:

> She was living as the remaining old families lived. She, whose life once had been in palatial mansions with fleets of servants, wound up in one shabby third floor room of a house in old Frenchtown, where she shared a kitchen and bath with seven others. One or two pieces of furniture and some old family photographs that she managed to retrieve were the lonely links to her past life.[63]

In this tight space, which she shared with seven others, Daisy held court with her English students and an increasing number of reporters interested in her story: pouring tea, telling stories, modelling English conversation for her students who were starved of other opportunities for hearing and testing their English pronunciation. Many found Daisy exotic, drawn to her 'Australian' background and Western ways, often projecting onto her a mixed-race Chinese-Caucasian identity. Her visitors 'could never believe Daisy was 100% Chinese', Tess Johnston wrote, 'and always complimented her on her fine grasp of the Chinese language, when they were not admiring her flawless English'.[64]

One of her students remembered: 'We spoke to her in English, because she is an English teacher and also because she is more used to English.' Although she had lived in China for more than seventy years, 'she had a thick, steady and mellow voice coming from her chest, which was quite different from the voice of a normal old lady in Shanghai'. Her Australian accent had faded over time:

> She was sent to McTyeire School to study and at that time spoke with an Australian accent, having a large emphasis on the 'A' sound. Now she does not speak with that accent. She never noticed whether that was corrected during the years at McTyeire School, or during the later years when she was studying at Yenching University.[65]

At some point in the early 1980s Daisy made contact with the newly reopened Australian consulate in Shanghai.[66] Evan Williams, an official at the consulate in Shanghai who encountered her in early 1986, remembers a 'slight woman with grey hair who told fantastic stories'.[67] Tess Johnston recalls meeting Daisy at the consulate happy hour: 'People seemed to cluster around her and I said, who is that, and people said that's Daisy Kwok. And they said, "oh she is from the Wing On Department Store fortune and she never left China".'[68] At a time when the foreign population of Shanghai was tiny – around 150 people, most of whom were Japanese – Daisy was, in Evan Williams' words, 'mixing with us at a time when it wouldn't have gone unnoticed'.[69] At the consulate Daisy worked as a teacher and translator. She was one of a select group of teachers circulating in diplomatic circles at the time. Some would impart their knowledge of pre-1949 Shanghai during lessons. One instructor was famous for teaching his students Chinese and tap dancing, having worked as a jazz musician before 1949. Above all, these individuals were useful reminders of China's pre-1949 connections with the West at a time when newly arrived diplomats were re-establishing a foreign presence in the country.

They also served as a repository of knowledge for overseas Chinese families seeking out their ancestral ties to a newly accessible mainland. By then, a younger generation of the Kwok family who were living abroad frequently visited Shanghai and Daisy took them to see the old house in Lucerne Road.[70] At that time thirty-seven families were housed there. Tess Johnston remembered visiting the house with Daisy: 'I asked her where the servants' quarters were and she said she didn't know. I think that says a lot about her old life, and the fall she experienced after 1949.'[71] Chen Danyan writes of the late 1980s and early 1990s as a time of restoration and nostalgia for Shanghai's more cosmopolitan Republican-era past. At a time of 'reform and opening', foreign connections and capitalist success were celebrated once more. During the 1990s, when Shanghai began to be restored to much of its former self, an old photo of Daisy's family, taken in front of their large house, was featured in many publications. One author mentioned that during the 1990s, when the economy was booming and the rich were buying villas and cars, the Kwok mansion in the picture should have been called 'Back to the Future . . . When Shanghai people looked at the photo they could not determine whether they had returned to the past or arrived in the future.'[72]

Daisy died on 25 September 1998. She donated her remains to the Red Cross Society. Family members speculated that seeing her parents' graves vandalised, and eventually dug up, during the Cultural Revolution motivated this decision. The Australian consul general, Murray McLean, spoke at her funeral. Officials from the Overseas Chinese Office said that they had only just learnt she was a Chinese Australian who had returned to China as a child. She had never mentioned this to them.[73]

* * *

So now I return to my original question in Chapter 1: how do we read Chinese Australian journeys to Shanghai across the long twentieth century? Since her death, Daisy's story has been canonised in the field of overseas Chinese history by one of its founders, Wang Gungwu, who first heard about her as a small boy living in the Malay fishing village of Ipoh:

> relatives of family friends arrived as refugees from the Japanese invasion of China [in 1937]. They had come from Shanghai where they were all born. I found them very different from the rest of us and their memories very fresh and exciting. Through the eldest of them, I met a strong longing for the home he had left. Together we learnt patriotic songs about the war in China, went to tearful Chinese films, and read lively Shanghai magazines. But what struck me most was his admiration for an aunt who stayed on in Shanghai.

Wang's relatives had smuggled Daisy's documents and photograph albums out of China. This decision would preserve Daisy's youth in the glamorous sepia tones of interwar portraiture and her image would circulate, without her knowledge, throughout the overseas Chinese diaspora for decades to come. And as it did, her photographs acquired a revered status – relics from a lost city now out of reach to many families. After Daisy's death, Chen Danyan would travel around the world collecting copies of the photographs to place in Daisy's memoir. Daisy herself witnessed the remainder of her photograph collection destroyed by Red Guards – she only managed to preserve one wedding photo, which she gave to Tess Johnston in the 1990s. As a young boy looking at these albums in the 1940s, Wang found the images affecting:

> I was shown photographs of her wedding to his [Wang Gungwu's friend's] uncle. She was radiant in a beautiful wedding gown that would have drawn sighs from brides-to-be in London and Paris. I learnt that she was born of Cantonese parents in Sydney and had grown up with English as her first language. Her father founded a department store in Sydney and the success of that venture led him to establish similar stores in Hong Kong and Shanghai. These stores grew to be part of an international chain that had pride of place in the business history of modern China. Following the success, the aunt moved to Shanghai and made that her home. To my friend, she was the epitome of all that was modern and progressive, and symbolized the China that he wanted to see flourish. In today's terms, she was transnational before the word was invented.[74]

In the 1990s he was sent a copy of Daisy's memoirs and reflected on his reaction:

> I was particularly moved when I read about how his aunty felt about the death of her husband in the hands of fanatical Communist youth, and why she stayed on in Shanghai to dedicate herself to teaching English to another generation. She continued to do so into her eighties, until a few years before she died. Every page of the book added to my understanding of how this daughter of Sydney, despite all that happened to her and her family, came to love Shanghai.

For Wang, Daisy's life could be firmly plotted into a grander narrative of overseas Chinese nationalism, a way to knit together a resilient tie to a Chinese homeland across distinct historical epochs. This interpretation of Daisy's story builds upon a foundation already set by the editor of her memoirs, Chen Danyan, who spent considerable time depicting Daisy as a Chinese patriot who had chosen to stay in Shanghai while almost every other member of her wealthy family had fled.[75]

Viewing mobile Australians in the interwar years beyond the heuristic context of empire allows us to break down monolithic readings of European empires and the place of 'Australians' within these empires. The fragments of Chinese Australian family histories collected here reveal a skein of interconnected lives, rooted simultaneously in Shanghai, Australia and the wider world.[76] These journeys can go some way to balancing histories that emphasise the often-thwarted attempts of Chinese migrants to enter Australia, rather than Chinese Australian desires to migrate to China. As Kate Bagnall has argued, there is a need to reimagine the migratory relationship between Australia and China through models that take into account the actions of Australians 'who maintained strong family or business connections with the Chinese communities in Australia or with those in China itself'.[77] These families were involved in many of the key moments in Australian and Chinese history and their lives were imbricated in the move away from empire and towards Asian decolonisation. Within their family histories we can trace the melding of cultural practices, alongside the struggles of interracial marriage, the renegotiation of previous identities as regimes shifted and the politicisation of family intimacy during the treaty port years, the Cold War, the Cultural Revolution and the period of Opening and Reform.

Notes

1 Nien Cheng, *Life and Death in Shanghai* (New York: Grove Press, 1987), 35.
2 Catherine Ladds, 'Eurasians in Treaty-Port China: Journeys across Racial and Imperial Frontiers', unpublished chapter, 17. I am grateful to the author for sharing her work with me prior to publication.
3 On the ending of the foreign presence in China after 1949 see: B. Hooper, *China Stands Up: Ending the Western Presence, 1948–50* (London: Allen & Unwin, 1986) and J. Howlett, '"Decolonisation" in China, 1949–59', in R. Bickers and J. Howlett (eds.) *Britain and China, 1840–1970: Empire, Finance and War* (Abingdon: Routledge, 2015), 222–241; Sherman Cochrane, *Encountering Chinese Networks: Western, Japanese, and Chinese Corporations in China, 1880–1937* (Berkeley: University of California Press, 2000).
4 Letter from E. Winsall, Director of the Relief Bureau of the International Red Cross, Geneva, to A. W. H. Wilkinson, Foreign Office, London, enclosing a report, 'The Situation of Foreign Refugees in Shanghai', 11 March 1952, TNA, FO 371/99374, FC 1822/38.
5 See: Wing On and Sincere Co. Enemy Property Committee, 1943, Nanjing Second Archives 二零零二(2)-535. My thanks to Michael Williams for this reference.
6 'The Late Mr Kwok Bew', *North China Herald*, 6 January 1932.
7 'Eulogy for Mavis Gock Yen'. My thanks to Richard and Siaomen Horsburgh for kindly sharing this with me.
8 Ibid.
9 C. H. Wu, *Dollars Dependents and Dogma; Overseas Chinese Remittances to Communist China* (Stanford, CA: Hoover Institution on War, Revolution and Peace, 1967), 81: 'there were virtually no remittances . . . and most of the dependents lived in areas occupied by the Japanese'. I am grateful to Michael Williams for this reference.
10 'Interview with Evelyn Yin Lo', CoSA Shirley Fitzgerald papers (SFP).
11 Glen Peterson, *Overseas Chinese in the People's Republic of China* (Hong Kong: Taylor & Francis, 2012). See also: Glen Peterson, 'House Divided: Transnational Families in the Early Years of the People's Republic of China', *Asian Studies Review* 31 (2007): 25–40.
12 B. C. Wall, Commonwealth Immigration Officer, to the Secretary of the Department of Immigration, Canberra, 'Pearl Kwok Fu (Pearl Bew) – Application for Passport – 50/1/1149', 28 June 1950, NAA SP244/2 N1950/2/3885.

13 Chen Danyan, *Shanghai Princess* (陈丹燕著，上海的金枝玉叶) (Taibei Shi: Erya chubanshe, 1999), 108.

14 Daisy Kwok draft memoirs, 'Materials Relating to Daisy Kwok', Tess Johnston papers, HI, 2015C32, Box 17, Folder 5.

15 See: Wing On and Sincere Co. Enemy Property Committee, 1943.

16 Ibid.

17 Chen, *Shanghai Princess*, 117.

18 Ibid.

19 Sherman Cochrane, 'Capitalists Choosing Communist China: The Liu Family of Shanghai, 1948–1956', in Jeremy Brown and Paul G. Pickowicz (eds.) *Dilemmas of Victory: The Early Years of the People's Republic of China* (Cambridge, MA: Harvard University Press, 2007), 369. See also: Joseph W. Esherick, 'The Ye Family in New China', in Brown and Pickowicz (eds.) *Dilemmas of Victory*, 311–337.

20 Email correspondence with Siaomen Horsburgh.

21 Siu-Lun Wong, *Emigrant Entrepreneurs* (Hong Kong: Oxford University Press, 1988), 188.

22 'Interview with Evelyn Yin Lo', SFP.

23 'Interview with Daphne Lowe', SFP, SFO480.

24 'Materials Relating to Daisy Kwok', Tess Johnston papers, HI, 2015C32, Box 17, Folder 5.

25 'Driving Miss Daisy', Tess Johnston, draft obituary for Daisy Kwok's funeral, 'Materials Relating to Daisy Kwok'.

26 Chen, *Shanghai Princess*, 131.

27 Ibid., 143.

28 'My son, Leonard Zhong Zheng Woo', Daisy Kwok draft memoirs'.

29 'Driving Miss Daisy'.

30 Peterson, *Overseas Chinese in the People's Republic of China*, 312.

31 'The Cultural Revolution', Daisy Kwok draft memoirs.

32 Daisy Kwok draft memoirs.

33 'The Cultural Revolution', Daisy Kwok draft memoirs.

34 Daisy Kwok draft memoirs.

35 Ibid.

36 Ibid.

37 'Miss Kwok', 'Materials Relating to Daisy Kwok'.

38 Daisy Kwok draft memoirs.

39 Ibid.

40 Ibid.

41 Chen Danyan, 'Secrets of a Survivor in the Face of Adversity', *Xinhua News*, 20 November 1996. See also: 'Daisy Refused to Wilt as Old Shanghai Changed', *Deseret News*, 26 July 1996.

42 Author interview with Tess Johnston, Shanghai, 8 October 2014.

43 'Thousands Slain in China's Red Purge', *SMH*, 20 August 1951.

44 Peterson, *Overseas Chinese in the People's Republic of China*.

45 On 14 December 1951 a letter signed by over 1,100 Chinese in the US was sent to Mao Zedong and the Overseas Chinese Affairs Commission accusing the People's Republic of widespread violations of overseas Chinese lives and property. 'If this is liberation', wrote the signatories, 'then it can only mean the annihilation of overseas Chinese families.' The Chinese Association of San Francisco eventually brought a petition condemning the PRC's attempts to 'extort' money from overseas Chinese before the United Nations. See: Peterson, *Overseas Chinese in the People's Republic of China*.

46 'China – Protection of Australian Embassy Nanking – Evacuation of Australian Embassy Staff', NAA A1838 494/1/20; 'Protection – Relief and Repatriation. Alice Rose Lim Sang', NAA A1068/IC47/20/1/11/9.

47 Confidential memo – Hong Kong Consulate Overwhelmed by Family Reunion Cases from Canton 9/4/1980, NAA A1838/332/3107/38/1/5 Part 3.
48 'Australians in China – Financial Relief – Lim, Mrs ARW', NAA A4144 18/194.
49 '"Herrenvolk" of Far East?', *Daily Mercury*, 13 February 1950, 7.
50 'Who Are the Overseas Chinese?', *Morning Bulletin*, 26 November 1954, 5. See also: 'Drought in Red China', *Canberra Times*, 31 May 1962; 'Red China Exports "Opium"', *Southern Cross*, 22 August 1952; 'Dissension in Red China', *World's News*, 11 August 1951; 'Mass Red Killings in China', *Courier Mail*, 4 April 1951.
51 Cheng, *Life and Death in Shanghai*, 35.
52 Ibid., 363.
53 Glen Peterson, 'Socialist China and the *Huaqiao*: The Transition to Socialism in Rural Guangdong, 1949–1956', *Modern China*, 14.3 (July 1988): 309–335.
54 It was not until 1978, with the publication of a report by party official Liao Chengzhi entitled 'We Must Pay Attention to Overseas Chinese Work' or *Bixu zhongshi qiaowu gongzuo*, that official attitudes towards domestic overseas Chinese like Daisy softened to allow many to be released from prison or mandatory re-education camps.
55 Author interview with Tess Johnston, Shanghai, 1 November 2014.
56 Email correspondence with Siaomen Horsburgh.
57 Chen, *Shanghai Princess*.
58 Ibid., 74.
59 Ibid.
60 'Driving Miss Daisy'.
61 Chen, *Shanghai Princess*, 23.
62 Cheng, *Life and Death in Shanghai*, 35.
63 'Driving Miss Daisy'.
64 Ibid.
65 'Miss Kwok', 'Materials relating to Daisy Kwok'.
66 Email correspondence with Murray Mclean and Evan Williams. See also: 'Alistair Murray McLean – Consul General of Shanghai', NAA A10476 TC-AM Part 5; 'China – Australian Representation – Australian Consulate General in Shanghai', NAA A1838 3107/38/1/5 Part 2.
67 Author interview with Evan Williams, 16 November 2014.
68 Tess Johnston interview, 1 November 2014.
69 Evan Williams interview.
70 Ibid.
71 Tess Johnston interview, 1 November 2014.
72 'Miss Kwok', 'Materials relating to Daisy Kwok'. See also: Chen, *Shanghai Princess*, 45.
73 'Materials Relating to Daisy Kwok'.
74 I am grateful to Mei-fen Kuo for bringing this reference to my attention. Wang Gungwu, 'Mixing Memory and Desire: Tracking the Migrant Cycles', in Tan Chee-Beng, Colin Storey and Julia Zimmerman (eds.) *Chinese Overseas: Migration, Research and Documentation* (Hong Kong: Chinese University Press, 2007), 3–22.
75 Chen, *Shanghai Princess*, 18.
76 Alison Blunt, '"Land of Our Mothers": Home, Identity, and Nationality for Anglo-Indians in British India, 1919–1947', *History Workshop Journal* 54 (2002): 49–72.
77 Kate Bagnall, 'A Journey of Love: Agnes Breuer's Sojourn in 1930s China', in Desley Deacon, Penny Russell and Angela Woollacott (eds.) *Transnational Ties: Australian Lives in the World* (Canberra: ANU ePress, 2008), 125.

Part II

Finding Work in the Eastern Markets

3 Work and Surveillance in Australian Expatriate Communities

Each treaty port had its cohort of foreign drifters, stranded sailors and pitiful failures.[1]
Albert Feuerwerker, 'The Foreign Presence in China'

In late 1934 a small fire broke out in an attic in Shanghai. Firemen would later testify in court that the fire was caused not by the usual gas leak or faulty wiring but, rather, by the presence of 'elaborate equipment for manufacturing and selling narcotics'.[2] After seizing large amounts of opium, along with cocaine and heroin, police sought out the responsible party. On 9 January 1935 an Australian, Mrs Johnson, was charged in 'one of the most sensational cases in Shanghai's criminal history'.[3] Emphasising the seriousness of the case, the prosecution pointed out that 114 Chinese had recently been executed in the area for a similar offence under the newly promulgated narcotics suppression laws. By virtue of her British citizenship, Mrs Johnson escaped an equal sentence. Instead, she was deported back to Australia, the destination of much of the opium that she had been selling since 1933.[4] Chinese newspapers reported that Mrs Johnson had gone back to 'that place where the British sent their prisoners after the American War'. As Australian unemployment figures rose in the wake of the Great Depression, the 'descendants of these prisoners' were making their way to China to find work.[5] The *China Critic* reminded its readers that Mrs Johnson was just one of thousands of Australians in China in the 1930s. For the swelling numbers of Australians in treaty ports, the *China Critic* had the following message: 'To them we say "Go home and scatter all your white man's pride to the wind and remove your immigration discrimination against Asiatics and cultivate your goodwill for the Chinese people before you come to do business here".'[6] Australians must accept that: 'It is not for you to reform us, though you may think it is a "white man's burden".'[7]

The commercial activity of white Australians was of more than passing interest to Chinese readers. The case of Mrs Johnson was not just yet another example of the hypocrisy of imperial rule dispensing harsh punishments to Chinese residents and lenient sentences to Europeans. Nor was it simply proof that white Australians dealt in opium as commonly as did their Chinese counterparts. Rather, Mrs Johnson's contraband stood for, in Anna Tsing's words, the 'awkward, unequal, unstable and creative interconnection across difference' that occurs when economic transactions take on cultural significance.[8] Sitting at the nefarious end of a network of goods and people moving on ships between Shanghai and Sydney, Perth and Manila every week, Mrs Johnson's opium broke through the facade of Australians' national boundaries, its 'great white walls' and its isolation from Asia.[9] At a time when the White Australia Policy barred Asian migration to Australia, her trading exposed the divergence between the 'fixity celebrated by nation-builders and the hyperactive movement that was at the heart of the economy and culture of the colonial world'.[10] If Australians wanted to trade in Asia, and many economists thought Australia's recovery from economic depression depended on selling Australian goods in the Eastern markets, then how could Australian claims to racial superiority, economic protectionism and cultural isolation be sustained?

We have followed the Kwok family as they negotiated treaty port life as Chinese Australians from 1918. Their time in Australia would have taught them to value their freedom of mobility in Shanghai and their relationship with the relevant government authorities. In Sydney they could not vote or claim any kind of welfare and, if they married a Chinese citizen, they lost their Australian residency by forfeiting their certificate of naturalisation. But once in Shanghai they joined other returned overseas Chinese as Cantonese in Shanghai. Their Australian background was only relevant in white expatriate circles.[11]

The Great Depression brought a different Australian population into view in China. These were Australian economic migrants, seeking work and opportunity, and influenced by hackneyed press reports depicting Shanghai as the 'Paris of the East', a land of riches in easy reach of Australian port cities. Many came laden with expectations: that they would be welcomed by the British in Shanghai, their fellow empire builders; that they could trade on their racial superiority as white men and women; and that, above all, work and money would be easy to come by. As we shall see, these visions would come up jarringly against reality as the 1930s progressed.

In recent years historians have begun interrogating connections between anticolonial movements and the economic dislocations of the Great Depression.[12] Ann L. Foster's work on the United States and Europe in Southeast Asia (1919–1941) has shown that the Depression served as a catalyst for numerous uprisings that challenged the colonial order. Large numbers of plantation workers from Java, Sumatra, Borneo, India and China lost their livelihoods after the price of rubber, rice, sugar, kapok, pepper and coffee fell by up to 50 per cent.[13] In Nghe Tinh in Vietnam and in Saya San in Burma, protracted rebellions, involving thousands of people, began in 1930 and lasted until 1932; peasants staged demonstrations in front of the homes of French and British landowners, burnt down such symbols of power as pagodas and *dinh* (village communal temples), and intimidated local officials into relinquishing power.[14] More than 1,300 rebels were killed by British troops across Burma's twelve provinces and a further 125 were hanged for their participation.[15] Similar rebellions occurred in the Caribbean and in Africa between 1930 and 1932.[16] Pioneers of Indian Ocean historiography such as Sugata Bose have likewise established links between the Great Depression and anticolonial nationalism in India.[17]

While a link between Chinese anticolonialism and the Great Depression in Australia has not yet been made explicit, there is a changing historiography which positions interwar Australian history in a transnational frame. These new histories are especially attentive to global connections and knowledge transfers. Marilyn Lake and Henry Reynolds show that the intellectual currents shaping racial inequality flowed round the globe in the nineteenth and twentieth centuries, and that colonised peoples – from Australia to the United States, the Pacific, South Africa and India – responded to and shaped these currents.[18] Fiona Paisley's recovery of the transnational context of interwar Australian feminism through the Women's Pan Pacific Congress has equally emphasised the importance of global connections.[19] Angela Woollacott has traced the increased mobility of Australian women travelling between Australia and London in the 1930s seeking work, sexual freedom and personal fulfilment. Colonial experiences of modernity were constituted in such interaction, Woollacott argues, with implications for the reproduction of racial hierarchy: 'Whiteness travelled both discursively and materially between Australia and Britain, and its meanings were always reconfigured in these circulations.'[20] Being colonial, being white and being modern in the 1930s, therefore, was a transcolonial experience, understood by comparing and contrasting London and Australia, colony and metropole. Margaret Allen has uncovered the letters of Indian men, formerly resident in Australia, seeking to return to Australia after the passing of the Immigration Restriction Act in 1901. The fact that they were barred from doing so, she writes, reveals how white Australian expectations of mobility contrasted with the construction of Indians as having no right to mobility.[21] 'The mobility of modernity', she concludes, 'was reserved for those deemed white.'[22]

This book draws attention to Australia's Depression-era labour migrants and elevates this period as central to the history of China–Australia relations. Following white Australians travelling to Shanghai during the Great Depression, and the fate of the goods they peddled, provides but a small step in this direction. These journeys can go some way to balancing histories that emphasise the often-thwarted attempts of Chinese migrants to enter Australia, rather than white Australian desires to migrate to China. As Kate Bagnall has argued, there is a need to reimagine the migratory relationship between Australia and China through models which take into account the actions of white Australians 'who maintained strong family or business connections with the Chinese communities in Australia or with those in China itself'.[23] While Australian missionaries and tourists in Asia have received much attention in recent scholarship, salespeople, labourers and traders have not. This gap points to a tendency in Australian history to assume that white Australians travelling to China were motivated by non-economic concerns such as religious calling, family ties or a desire for adventure. Chinese migrants, on the other hand, are consistently depicted as travelling to Australia for materialistic reasons only; Australians in Asia were travellers and missionaries, Chinese in Australia were 'coolies' or labourers.

The circulation of poorer Australians around Asian port cities in the 1930s had clear effects on native populations. Depression-like conditions were felt in Australia from 1927 onwards. Thousands of unemployed left their communities to find work elsewhere as economic strains worsened and Australia experienced the worst effects of the Wall Street crash of 1929. The number of Australians in treaty port China grew so significantly that, by 1934, the Lyons government was forced to issue an official warning dissuading Australians from travelling there without first having obtained employment.[24] The British consul general in China had reported to the Commonwealth that 'unemployment amongst British subjects in Shanghai [was] so serious, that persons who were contemplating going there from Australia in search of work should be warned not to do so'.[25] Stowaways from Australia had been arriving in Shanghai but no work was available for them. The position had become desperate 'owing to the number of British subjects already in Shanghai who are unemployed'.[26] The British government asked the Lyons government 'to do what it can to stop Australians proceeding to China'.[27] By the mid-1930s an ANZAC relief society had been established in Shanghai and Hong Kong 'with the object of assisting Australians, particularly those who were destitute . . . providing them with their return passage money to Australia'. Its founder, Pete Eardley, 'warned Australians to think deeply before leaving for China on the prospect of securing work.'[28] We are not used to thinking of white Australians as sojourners moving between Australia and China, but in the 1920s and 1930s they did, and in significant numbers.

One result of this migration was the generation of a substantial archive in the files of the Shanghai Municipal Police (SMP) force. By 1930 Shanghai was the fifth biggest city in the world and its police force was substantial.[29] Formed in 1854 by British 'land renters' living in Shanghai under the extraterritorial provisions of the 1842 Treaty of Nanjing (the so-called 'Unequal Treaties'), the SMP was administered by the British-run Shanghai Municipal Council.[30] Isabella Jackson argues that the SMP was the most potent symbol of British imperial authority in Shanghai's changing political landscape in the 1930s, where 'Britain's formal and informal empires constantly overlapped and intersected', and where American and Japanese influence was on the ascendancy.[31] Thanks largely to the recent work of Bickers and Jackson, we now know a lot more about the men and women who staffed the Shanghai police force, the 'deskwallahs' or 'servants of empire', as Alan Lester and David Lambert have described them.[32] The SMP comprised British, Sikh and Chinese officers with rates of pay defined by ethnicity, not aptitude.[33] While Sikh constables were recruited directly from the Punjab, from 1885 Chinese constables were principally from northern China, local men being seen as inferior. British recruits were brought directly from England.[34] As the numbers of destitute Australians in Shanghai grew in the 1920s and 1930s, so too did the number of dossiers on Australians in the 'special branch' files of the SMP archives. The special branch of the SMP was charged with providing an orderly environment for Shanghai's foreign trade and commerce. Carrying out its duties required 'the timely gathering of information on areas of potential instability that might threaten Shanghai's economic development'.[35] The period covered by these files extends from 1894 to 1945 and the special branch dossier files, which date from 1929 to 1945, provide the most extensive coverage.

European claims to sovereignty under the treaty port system were tenuous and unclear, and British extraterritoriality in Shanghai was no exception.[36] With the end of the Opium War in 1842, Shanghai began a 106-year period of foreign occupation, described as 'semi-colonialism'. European powers leased or were ceded land to the city's north and west, laying the base for what was to become known as the International Settlement and the French Concession. Recognisably European settlements with distinctively Western architectural features evolved rapidly, eventually overwhelming the old Chinese city. The original intention was to exclude Chinese and other foreigners from this area, and the first set of land regulations in 1845 prohibited the native inhabitants from selling or renting land or houses.[37] Other foreigners, however, claimed the right under Article 8 of the Treaty of the Bogue to rent land on the same terms as the English so that the British settlement became occupied by those of all nationalities.[38] The number of foreigners grew rapidly in Shanghai, reaching 100,000 by 1930.[39] While Chinese were initially excluded from the International Settlement, by 1915 more than 620,000 were living there.[40] Although it was by no means implied in the text of the treaties that the foreigners should be allowed to set up their own municipal administration in the areas set apart for their residence, 'the convention was firmly implanted and had been acted upon during two-hundred years of intercourse at Canton that the foreigners should be responsible for managing their own affairs'.[41] From this same idea sprang extraterritoriality, a slippery diplomatic invention and derogation of Chinese sovereignty. The establishment of a police force on Chinese territory, and in the presence of treaties whereby the Emperor of China had guaranteed protection to the strangers within his gates, was recognised by international law to be 'strictly speaking untenable'.[42] Shanghai was not a colony like Hong Kong, but the Chinese in Shanghai were treated like colonial subjects.[43] European communities in Shanghai justified the existence of institutions such as the SMP with arguments anchored in the urban landscape; the Europeans had 'made Shanghai', they argued, and now European forms of governance, including the police force, helped keep the city stable through a commitment to 'law and order' and the delivery of 'a higher standard of living'.[44]

Special branch officers from the SMP began surveillance on some Australian suspects from the 1920s, resulting in a rare glimpse of the day-to-day life of these men and women through urban streetscapes, into cabaret bars and up staircases to boarding houses. Within the pages of these files are newspaper cuttings spanning publications from London, Shanghai, Hong Kong, Durban and Melbourne in both Chinese and English.

It is worth pausing here to comment on the somewhat ambiguous distinction between 'Australians' and 'Britons' in the interwar years. Historians have established that most Australians identified themselves as 'British' in the first half of the twentieth century. 'In-so-far as they were members of a "white" Dominion,' argues Lachlan Strahan, 'most Australians in Shanghai still saw themselves as

Britishers.'[45] How then were local Chinese or SMP officers to distinguish an 'Australian' from an 'Englishman'? While some Australians might have been unwilling or unlikely to call themselves 'Australian', SMP officers took a different view, clearly identifying suspects as Australian and not British. They were not alone. Other sections of Shanghai's population (White Russians or Jewish refugees for example), and for the purposes of this chapter the local Chinese majority, regularly drew distinctions between Britons and Australians. Some Australians, including, for example, Victorian horse salesman Rex Phillips, arrived in Shanghai as 'British' but later identified as Australian after being excluded from British social circles where he was referred to as a *mafoo* (a stable hand).[46] As we saw in Chapter 1, some Australians remedied this situation by simply pretending to be British.

Australians themselves used nationalism to demarcate treaty port life. Lachlan Strahan writes that Australian diplomat Frederic Eggleston drew a clear line between Australian and British diplomats when it came to their engagement with the Chinese environment in which they were living: 'They [British diplomats] are capable of living in a country and not altering one jot their method of life, and of betraying little interest in the country in which they are living.'[47] For Strahan, Egglestone was a 'transitional figure standing between an automatic affinity with all things British, and a more independent Australian outlook'.[48] Egglestone's colleague Keith Waller was even more critical: 'The Chinese have had considerable experience of the Treaty Port Englishman who thought that he was only a little lower than the angels and a good deal more important.'[49]

The ways in which the word 'Australian' was invoked in these cases highlights the crucial role played by class divisions in the construction of colonial categories in Chinese treaty ports, as well as the politics of location in the generation of colonial cultures. Privilege and whiteness in Shanghai were never exclusively racial prerogatives. Chinese newspapers, for example, in their reporting of Mrs Johnson's arrest for narcotics dealing, were quick to point out her Australian-ness and the convict associations of this Australian-ness ('that place where the British sent their prisoners after the American War').

There has been much debate among scholars as to the proper definition of British imperialism in China.[50] Chinese historians have traditionally used the Maoist/Marxist definition of 'semi-colonialism', but some have begun recently to reconsider the nature of semi-colonialism in China's treaty ports.[51] Ruth Rogaski has coined the term 'hyper-colony' for the treaty port of Tianjin.[52] 'Tianjin's status as a hyper-colony', she argues, 'placed Chinese urban dwellers under the gaze – and sometimes the control – of several different imperial powers. At the same time this condition offered the Chinese a perspective on several variant models of urban modernity and colonial ideology.'[53] By invoking the term 'Australian' and by rejecting Australian goods, Chinese locals in Shanghai allow us to view the complexity of local Chinese agency in a hyper-colonial context. This use of the term 'Australian' further reveals how national categories of difference functioned against and in the service of colonial categories. Fan'ti Fan has suggested the term 'cultural borderlands' as a way of formulating the overlap of conflicting nationalist, colonial and cultural categories in Chinese treaty port contexts. 'As historical investigators we should not leave such conventional categories as East/West and Chinese/European unexamined,' Fan argues, '[f]or these were not fixed entities, but products of boundary drawing and power negotiations among historical actors.'[54] Therefore, when historical subjects employed such cognitive categories as Chinese, Australian or white to classify themselves, Fan argues, we should ask how they defined these categories and how these categories became stabilised in a particular historical context.[55] Some Australians in Shanghai found their claims to racial and cultural superiority in dispute. So too was the 'modernity' of the goods they had for sale. Chinese newspapers depicted Australian goods as poor quality, 'backward' and undesirable.[56] Some Chinese consumers refused to buy Australian products, citing the White Australia Policy as a form of imperialist humiliation directed towards Chinese citizens. For some Chinese journalists in Shanghai, invoking the category of 'Australian' denoted convict characteristics and criminality and was a form of anticolonial critique against British imperialism. Reports in Australian newspapers about the difficulties experienced by unemployed Australians in China were critical of Australian attitudes towards Chinese migrants and argued that Australian modernisation and industrialisation depended on trade with the East.[57]

Rumours circulated by salespeople themselves, both in Shanghai and on their return to Australia, made their way into government memoranda, alarming policymakers bent on conquering the 'Eastern markets'. The existence of dispersed archives, in both Australia and China, provides a means by which I can address one of the pervading tensions of empire in interwar Australia: the relationship between working-class aspirations for social mobility and the exclusionary and discriminatory practices of white settler societies. The conflicted encounters of the individuals that I trace through these archives suggest that the relationship between being modern and being colonial between the wars was co-constituted in both Australia and Asia. The impact of Australian activities on local Asian populations highlights the need to 'reintegrate national postcolonial histories into a broader imperial framework'.[58]

***

Phyllis Dowling was a country girl who some thought 'would never do much good'.[59] She was seventeen and had come from Condobolin to Sydney. She first stayed with her sister at Lindfield but later moved to a boarding house at 98 Victoria Street, Woolloomooloo. On 16 September 1916 two older women, Maud Nicol, aged 36, and May Camps, 27, were charged with conspiracy to procure Phyllis to become a common prostitute. Nicol had met Phyllis for lunch at the top of William Street and there had outlined their plan. The *Changsha* was about to leave for Shanghai and she hoped Phyllis would agree to go aboard, in order to join the household of one Miss Hooper in Shanghai, where 'wonderful and rich times' were promised.[60]

Long before the Great Depression, the clandestine movements of aspiring Chinese Australians and Australians like Phyllis Dowling linked Australia and treaty port China in a commercial network from below, often invisible in official diplomatic accounts of the period. Steamship services between Australia and Asian entry ports such as Shanghai dated back to 1831, although regular passenger services did not begin until the 1850s.[61] By the 1920s the three best-known steamships moving between the Australian east coast and China were the *Taiping*, the *Changte* and the *Changsha*, advertised on postcards and posters to be found pasted on the street corners of Woolloomooloo or behind glass frames in Shanghai hotel lobbies (see Figure 3.1).[62] These lines were primarily supported by the passenger trade made possible by Chinese Australian movement between China and Australia, but by the 1920s an increasing number of white Australians were also making these journeys

While many Australians may have feared an invasion of 'yellow' workers from China in the 1920s, there were a great many who had no such concerns about travelling in the opposite direction themselves, legally or otherwise, especially to prosperous port towns like Shanghai. For those Australians in contact with wharf labourers such as brothel madams Maud Nicol and May Camps, information about the movements, cargo and personnel of the *Changsha* and *Taiping* was easy to procure, and stowaways on these routes were common. The tangle of streets that spread upwards from Australian wharf districts (Woolloomooloo in Sydney, the Docklands in Melbourne) were dotted with popular brothels, the destination of some of Mrs Johnson's narcotics, which came off the *Changsha* in 1933. French and American sailors working on the Sydney–Manila–Shanghai–Kobe route told journalist Henry Champly in 1932 that they regularly helped women get to Shanghai.[63] 'They're ex-shop girls and ex-typists,' Marcel B. told Champly, '[these] women, I know how to talk to them.'[64] For anyone interested in making the journey, interwar Shanghai promised adventure and escape but also economic opportunity. 'Girl's Million Dollar Job' read an article in the *Sydney Morning Herald* in 1927: 'Girl bank clerk who reached Sydney on Saturday in the liner *Eastern* has just come from a job in Shanghai where she earned £37 a month! She did her shopping in suitcases!'[65]

Australia's early nation builders feared potential contamination – physical, cultural and commercial – brought about by interactions between white Australians and Asian peoples.[66] But, like many of the possibilities set up by settler colonial nationalism, these nation builders could not control the unpredictable ways in which commercial relationships took shape post-Federation. Raelene Frances's work on prostitution and the White Australia Policy has revealed how Australian authorities used their arbitrary power under the policy to control the movements of not only racial others but also women deemed to be prostitutes, proof of 'the increasingly narrow definition of White Australia between the world wars'.[67] As Frances has shown, officials were shocked at the number of women connected to prostitution rings who moved in and out of Australia in the 1920s and 1930s, some on their way to Shanghai.[68]

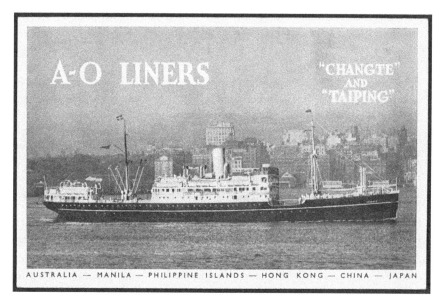

Figure 3.1 A&O Liners *Changte* and *Taiping*, postcard, *c.*1930.

Source: State Library of Victoria, H95.53/7.

Rumours of work in Shanghai circulating in wharf districts intersected with more official information about treaty port Asia provided by business magazines such as *Rydge's Business Journal* and monographs published by the Institute of Pacific Relations. *Rydge's* in particular had a wide circulation and was available at Salvation Army Halls, employment bureaus and YMCA offices in Australian cities and townships. As David Walker has shown, the early twentieth century saw calls for the development of a marketing culture in Australia, sensitive to the changing tastes and requirements of Asian consumers and able to tap into the fascination with the close and alluring Eastern markets.[69] A sharp rise in unemployment in Australia after 1927, when the price of wool and wheat plummeted, made the exploration of these new 'frontiers of trade' all the more pressing.[70] There was 'a wave of optimism regarding the future of Australia's commerce with the Far East', wrote John Shepherd in his 1939 Institute of Pacific Relations monograph *Australia's Interests and Policies in the Far East*.[71]

Certain China watchers had been calling for increased trade between Australia and China since the 1910s. When G. E. Morrison travelled on the SS *Akira Maura* from Sydney to Shanghai via Yokahama in 1917, he was shocked at the ignorance of Australian commercial travellers towards a potential China trade:

> The ship is filled with commercial travellers returning from a round trip to Japan. None of them have been to China proper although a few stayed over in Shanghai and one or two visited Canton. One man informed me last night

of the impossibility of buying amber and showed me an imitation cigarette holder which he had purchased for 10,000 yen in Japan. He was most astonished when I told him amber was one of the most widely distributed products of China. Another man who had been to Japan to purchase drugs was astonished when I told him how great were the possibilities for the purchase of drugs in China. He had a copy of the *Far Eastern Review* he had read with some pride. He represents Felton & Grimwalde, Melbourne. I enjoined him upon the necessity of advertising in the *Far Eastern Review* as well as buying it. Why not take up this case and write a series of papers upon the possible interchange of products and possibility of their sale in the China market? Ignorance is, as I told you before, colossal on both sides. Felton & Grimwalde have products just as popular as Pink Pills for Pale People for sale and if they only realised the vast fortunes to be made by pills they would not neglect China.[72]

Morrison's frustration at Australian ignorance of China's economic potential led him to write several letters to political and commercial organisations in Australia calling for a change in attitude. Once Chinese Australians had proved the potential of the China market through companies such as Wing On, Morrison had a strong precedent to point to in his advocacy of a China trade.

The Australian government eventually set up a Federal Advisory Committee on Eastern Trade in 1928 and sent Sir Herbert Gepp, founder of the Commonwealth Scientific and Industrial Research Organisation (CSIRO) and the government's chief adviser on industrialisation and modernisation, to Hong Kong and Shanghai.[73] In 1930 H. Gordon Bennett joined a cacophony of voices in *Rydge's Business Journal* urging Australians to try their luck in Asian treaty ports: 'The treaty ports of China are not only residential; they are distributing centres for foreign trade', Bennett told readers.[74] He described 'privileged conditions for Australians' in cities where guidance from white colonists was not only welcome but also needed: 'Under foreign guidance railways have been built, mines dug, factories opened and companies formed.'[75] Frank Clune agreed with this assessment when he visited Shanghai in 1939, telling his readers that the West was lifting China out of 'Asian sloth', providing much needed technological assistance.[76] As Maud Nicol and May Camps assured Phyllis Dowling before she boarded the *Changsha*, 'wonderful and rich times' awaited.

John Latham agreed, telling the Australian parliament upon his return from China in 1934, as part of the Australian Goodwill Mission report, that:

> It is obvious that our economic destiny, in which is wrapped the standard of living of our people, is already largely determined, and will be more largely in the future, by the volume of trade we do with countries in the East. The world today is passing through very difficult times.[77]

Latham, who was shown Shanghai by the Australian-born managers of the Nanjing Road department stores, called into question Australian perceptions of

China: 'From our childhood we have been accustomed to read, think and speak of the "Far East". It is the Far East to Europe, to the old centres of civilization, but we must realise it is the "Near East" to Australia.' He also warned of a future in which Australia would be dependent on the region:

> We are apt to think of the world as old, aged and worn. That may be. But the greater chance is that we are only in the beginning of human history today. We have to look forward not merely to next year and the year after, but also, I hope, to many centuries of a happy and prosperous civilization in this continent. It is inevitable that the relations between Australia and the Near East will become closer and more intimate as the years pass. Therefore it is important that we should endeavour to develop and improve our relations with our near neighbours whose fortunes are so important to us, not only in economic matters, but also in relation to vital issues of peace and war.[78]

Despite these exhortations to forge closer China ties, Latham also went on to praise the successes of the White Australia Policy: 'I am glad that we are essentially a European community and are not confronted by the problems that arise from mixed races in other parts of the world.'[79] As Latham's speech suggests, at the very time Australia was involved in an immense nation-building project through racial exclusion, Australia's economy was increasingly dependent on new markets in China. These tensions would become increasingly untenable. As J. H. C. Sleeman put it in 1933: 'The very first essential to us successfully trading in the East is to play the game. Then we have to jettison a little of our overweening racial vanity. If we don't, well, then we will deserve all that is coming to us.'[80] Upton-Close agreed in his bestseller *The Revolt in Asia*:

> Australia is not in a curious position. More and more Australians of all classes are beginning to see the star of trade rising in the East, but the East having simmered over a long period is beginning to boil like the broth in a witches' cauldron . . . The Chinese community in Australia should be used to full capacity to make contact.[81]

Even in the depths of the Great Depression, freighters and passenger boats were constantly coming and going from Shanghai: they entered China by the mouth of the Yangtze and then turned into the Whangpoo River, around which the city sprawled.[82] Shanghai in the 1930s was a confusing place 'with the most complex system of local government imaginable'.[83] Its physical layout, social composition, industry and government structures were all products of China's encounter with nineteenth-century imperialism. Before the Western incursion in the nineteenth century, it was a modestly prosperous regional capital with a growing importance as an entrepôt in the interregional trade with Jiangnan – a fertile, wealthy region south of the lower reaches of the Yangtze River, in which Shanghai itself was located. Physically, it was a small, walled town that had no room to accommodate foreigners, who were permitted to reside there from 1842, following the Opium

Figure 3.2 Scene on a wharf in Shanghai, 1920–1930.

Source: Bishop, Joseph and Family Collection, University of Melbourne Archives UMA/1/4545.

War. The foreign powers, therefore, leased what became known as the International Settlement. Recognisably European areas with distinctively Western architectural features evolved with remarkable rapidity, eventually overwhelming the old Chinese city in size and importance.[84] Spatial divisions within the city reflected colonial hierarchies and were enforced on the basis of race. These racially defined barriers were stronger in Shanghai than, for example, in Sumatra and were reinforced by social and sexual taboos.[85] For over sixty years, most Chinese were barred from Shanghai's parks, administered by the Shanghai Municipal Council. Rumours circulated that one sign outside Huangpu Park read 'Chinese and Dogs Not Admitted', an insult which took on particular potency in translation as the phrase 'dog' (*gou*) already had racist overtones in Chinese, having long been used by Han Chinese to deride members of ethnic minorities.[86]

The population of Shanghai at large, including the foreign concessions, was overwhelmingly Chinese, but the Chinese themselves were a highly diversified group. True natives of Shanghai were rare. This was pre-eminently an immigrant city, and the Chinese clustered in occupational and residential groups characterised by regional origin and dialect. The wealthy merchants were typically from Canton and Ningpo; the rickshaw drivers, street girls and gangsters were more likely to be from districts north of the Yangtze. The former lived alongside wealthy foreigners in the French Concession, the latter alongside poor foreigners in Hongkew – in the northern part of the International Settlement – or further away in Chapei, which was under Chinese local government. These 'poor foreigners' were mostly White Russians, rendered stateless by the Bolshevik Revolution, and later Jewish refugees fleeing Nazi-occupied Europe. As Robert Bickers has argued, the Chinese were quite alive to the quasi-colonial pecking order in Shanghai, and some learnt to 'scorn the stateless white Russians and Jewish refugees who were no better off than many of their poorer compatriots'.[87] Joining this awkward population of 'poor foreigners' during the 1920s and 1930s was a rapidly expanding community of white Australians.

While Depression-era Shanghai was, indeed, a city in which to buy and sell, it was also a place in which the act of sale and purchase was riddled with subtle colonial and anticolonial meanings. The successful development of Shanghai's commerce and industry, and society and culture, required engagement, cohabitation and dialogue between Chinese and Western elites in the city.[88] But by the 1920s and 1930s, boycotts of foreign 'imperialist' goods by Chinese student and union groups were growing increasingly common. An emerging consumer culture defined and spread modern Chinese nationalism through the National Products Movement, or *Guohuo Yundong*, which saw popular boycotts of Japanese and British products significantly damage the commercial operations of major foreign companies such as the British-American Tobacco Company.[89] China was not the only country to attempt to nationalise its consumer culture in the early twentieth century. The *swadeshi* and non-cooperation movements in India (1904–1908, 1920–1922) were also directed against imperialist rule. During the height of the National Products Movement in the 1930s, merchants who sold 'the national products of foreign devils' (*Yanguizi de Guohuo*) regularly had their shop windows smashed by radical student groups such as the Iron and Blood society.[90] Karl Gerth argues that popular nationalism in Republican-era China moulded a consumer culture by applying the categories of 'national', 'foreign' and 'imperial' to all commodities, creating in effect 'treasonous' and 'patriotic' products.[91] Such categories, Gerth suggests, had eugenic and racialised overtones. One participant in the Women's National Products Year of 1934 suggested that Chinese women who bought foreign goods should be labelled prostitutes because they degraded their bodies by 'consuming' imports.[92]

Gerth and Rogaski write of the National Products Movement as part of a wider 'moral fear' in China to do with perceptions of a 'Chinese deficiency', resulting from the view that the Chinese nation was the 'Sick Man of Asia'.[93] These views were most potently expressed in the New Life Movement, which aimed to 'regenerate' the Chinese people through the acceptance of commitment to a code of behaviour based on the Confucian virtues of Li (propriety), Yi (uprightness), Lian (integrity) and Chi (shame). These virtues found their practical application in all aspects of people's everyday lives, such as their choice of food, clothing, shelter and activities.[94] Proponents of the New Life Movement sought to improve Chinese sanitation and public manners in urban space ('spitting and burping in public', for example), making explicit a connection between 'orderly manners' and a strong Chinese nation capable of resisting imperialism. Politicians involved in the New Life Movement worried that trade deficits and 'new western consumer lifestyles exemplified by opium dens and addicts' perpetuated the image of China as backward, becoming a barrier to development and national 'strength'.[95] Intellectuals feared the loss of sovereignty implicit in the growing foreign dominance of the commercial economy.[96] The New Life Movement and the National Products Movement of the 1920s and 1930s articulated a grammar of modernity and citizenship in China, which found material form in boycotting British and 'empire' products and adhering to strict codes of behaviour in public areas.

Australians were thus arriving in China in large numbers at a time of heightened sensitivity among local Chinese over consumer choice, and growing belief that Western commodity culture in Chinese treaty ports symbolised lost sovereignty. The promoters of the 'Eastern markets' in Australia were accurate in their depiction of treaty port Shanghai as an economic hub. What their enthusiastic calls to trade failed to acknowledge, however, was the intensity and strength of Chinese anticolonial feeling in Shanghai, increasingly expressed through the agency of Chinese consumers. The boosters of Asian trade in Australia implied that Australians in China would be welcomed as civilisers. Not only would their labour be valued, one *Rydge's Business Journal* argued, but it would be a form of 'commercial intelligence'.[97] 'There is no commercial education in China – we can bring it', wrote J. R. Hinterland in 1931.[98] As Phillipa Levine has reminded us: 'Colonial assumptions about the west's role, or more literally the British role, as modernisers, and about the Orient as a corrupt and degraded backwater shaped around opposition' are fundamental to appreciating European imperial intervention in China.[99] Following the lives of Australians in Shanghai reveals the underlying tensions of empire in the twentieth century between working-class aspirations for social mobility through employment and opportunity and the racism at the heart of the settler colonial project. As the twentieth century progressed, Australia's economic claims in China would look to be on increasingly faulty ground, as anticolonialists, unionists and internationalists pointed to the contradiction between the racial exclusion of Asiatic peoples from the Australian nation and economic integration with Asian economies.

Notes

1 Albert Feuerwerker, 'The Foreign Presence in China', in J. K. Fairbank (ed.) *The Cambridge History of China, Volume 12: Republican China 1912–1949*, pt 1 (Cambridge: Cambridge University Press, 1986), 141.
2 'DRUG DEALING, Wife of Australian Charged, SHANGHAI SENSATION', *The Examiner*, 10 January 1935, 8.
3 'The Drug Traffic, Shanghai Sensation', *West Australian*, 10 January 1935, 15.
4 'DRUG DEALING, Wife of Australian Charged, SHANGHAI SENSATION', 8.
5 'Australia' (奧州)，*Eastern Magazine* (*Dongfang Zhouzhi*, 東方周知) 31.2 (1935): 47.
6 *China Critic* (*Zhongguo pinglun zhoukan*, 中國評論周刊), 27 August 1931, Shanghai Municipal Archives (SMA) D2-0-2237-22. The *China Critic* was founded on 31 May 1928 by a group of Chinese intellectuals who had studied in the United States and returned to China. Shuang Shen argues that the *China*

Critic's funding came directly from the Republican-era Nationalist government. See: Shuang Shen, *Cosmopolitan Publics: Anglophone Print Culture in Semi-Colonial Shanghai* (Piscataway, NJ: Rutgers University Press, 2009), 33.

7 *China Critic*, 27 August 1931, SMA D2-0-2237-22.

8 Anna Tsing, 'Introduction', in her *Friction: An Ethnography of Global Connection* (Princeton, NJ: Princeton University Press, 2005), 2.

9 Minutes of the Nation's Advisory Committee on Traffic in Opium and Other Dangerous Drugs, minutes of the twelfth session, held at Geneva 17 January to 2 February 1929 (Geneva: League of Nations, 1929); Joseph W. Esherick (ed.) *Remaking the Chinese City: Modernity and National Identity 1900–1950* (Honolulu: University of Hawai'i Press, 2000).

10 Tony Ballantyne, 'On Place, Space and Mobility in Nineteenth-Century New Zealand', *New Zealand Journal of History* 45.1 (2011): 66.

11 宋钻友 著 (Song Zuanyou zhu), 广东人在上海 (年) (Guangdong ren zai Shanghai [1843–1949]) (Shanghai: Shanghai renmin chubanshe, 2007).

12 Aric Putnam, 'Ethiopia Is Now: J.A. Rogers and the Rhetoric of Black Anti-colonialism during the Great Depression', *Rhetoric and Public Affairs* 10.3 (Fall 2007): 419–444; '"Blackbelt Millennium": Rhetorical Moments in Black Anti-colonial Nationalism during the Great Depression', PhD Thesis, University of Minnesota, July 2006; Ann L. Foster, *Projections of Power: The United States and Europe in Colonial Southeast Asia, 1919–1941* (Durham, NC: American Encounters/Global Interactions, Duke University Press, 2010).

13 Ann L. Foster, *Projections of Power*.

14 Ibid., 145.

15 Ibid., 147–148.

16 Christian Høgsbjerg, '"A Thorn in the Side of Great Britain": C. L. R. James and the Caribbean Labour Rebellions of the 1930s', *Small Axe* 15.3/36 (November 2011): 24–42.

17 Workshop held by Sugata Bose and Devleena Ghosh in the Transforming Cultures Centre at the University of Technology, Sydney, 12 September 2010. See also: Sugata Bose, *A Hundred Horizons: The Indian Ocean in the Age of Global Empire* (Cambridge, MA: Harvard University Press, 2006).

18 Marilyn Lake and Henry Reynolds, *Drawing the Global Colour Line: White Men's Countries and the Question of Racial Equality* (Melbourne: Melbourne University Press, 2008).

19 Fiona Paisley, *Glamour in the Pacific: Cultural Internationalism and Race Politics in the Women's Pan Pacific* (Honolulu: University of Hawai'i Press, 2009).

20 Angela Woollacott, *To Try Her Fortune in London: Australian Women, Colonialism and Modernity* (Oxford: Oxford University Press, 2001), 27.

21 Margaret Allen, 'Shadow Letters and the "Karnana" Letter: Indians Negotiate the White Australia Policy, 1901–21', *Life Writing* 8.2 (May 2011): 188.

22 Margaret Allen, '"Innocents abroad" and "Prohibited immigrants": Australians in India and Indians in Australia 1890–1910', in Ann Curthoys and Marilyn Lake (eds.) *Connected World: History in Transnational Perspective* (Canberra: ANU ePress, 2005), 113. See also: Margaret Allen, 'The Australian Horse Trader's Winter in Calcutta 1930', *JOSA Journal of the Oriental Society of Australia* 39–40, Part 1 (October 2008): 37–49; 'Shadow Letters and the "Karnana" Letter'; '"That's the Modern Girl": Missionary Women and Modernity in Calcutta, c.1907–c.1940', *Itinerario* 34.3 (2010): 83–96.

23 Kate Bagnall, 'A Journey of Love: Agnes Breuer's Sojourn in 1930s China', in Desley Deacon, Penny Russell and Angela Woollacott (eds.) *Transnational Ties: Australian Lives in the World* (Canberra: ANU ePress, 2008), 125.

24 'Not Wanted, Australian Stowaways, Warning from Shanghai', *Cairns Post*, 3 January 1934, 5; 'Keep Away from China: Australians Who Seek Work

Warned', *The Argus*, 3 January 1934, 5; 'Migrants to China, Government Warning, No Employment', *The Mercury*, 3 January 1934, 6; 'Unemployment Affects Britishers in China: Warning Issued', *Canberra Times*, 3 January 1934, 2; 'Unemployment in Shanghai, Warning to Australians', *West Australian*, 3 January 1934, 7.

25   'Unemployment in Shanghai, Warning to Australians', 7; 'Not Wanted, Australian Stowaways, Warning from Shanghai', 5.

26   'Keep Away from China: Australians Who Seek Work Warned', 5.

27   'Not Wanted, Australian Stowaways, Warning from Shanghai', 5.

28   'Much Distress in Shanghai: Anzac Society Asks for Help', *The Mercury*, 21 April 1938, 12; 'China–Shanghai–Future Status of International Settlement 1930–1938', NAA A981 CHIN 178.

29   Robert Bickers, *Empire Made Me: An Englishman Adrift in Shanghai* (London: Penguin Books, 2003), 40.

30   Robert Bickers, 'Shanghailanders: The Formation and Identity of the British Settler Community in Shanghai', *Past and Present* 159 (May 1998): 166.

31   Isabella Jackson, 'The Raj on Nanjing Road: Sikh Policeman in Treaty-Port Shanghai', *Modern Asian Studies* 46 (2012): 1. I am grateful to Isabella Jackson for generously sharing the manuscript of her article with me.

32   Bickers, *Empire Made Me*, 11; Jackson, 'The Raj on Nanjing Road'; David Lambert and Alan Lester, *Colonial Lives Across the British Empire: Imperial Careering in the Long Nineteenth Century* (Cambridge: Cambridge University Press, 2006).

33   Ibid., 5; by 1930 there were 511 European officers in the force, 691 Sikhs and 3,477 Chinese.

34   Ibid., 9.

35   'Jack Edward Ivers. Files on Noulens Associates: Jack Edward Ivers'. N.d. Shanghai Municipal Police Files, 1894–1945. US National Archives, Archives Unbound, Web, 1 March 2012. http://go.galegroup.com.rp.nla.gov.au/gdsc/i.do?&id=GALE%7CSC5100266094&v=2.1&u=nla&it=r&p=GDSC&sw=w&viewtype=fullcitation (accessed 2 March 2012).

36   P. K. Cassel, *Grounds of Judgment: Extraterritoriality and Imperial Power in Nineteenth-Century China and Japan* (Oxford: Oxford University Press, 2012).

37   'China – Foreign Concession', NAA A981/4 CHIN 61; 'China', NAA A981/4 CHIN 80 PART 2; 'Trade with China', NAA A595/2 BT1923/1195.

38   'China – Foreign Concession'.

39   Betty Peh-T'I Wei, *Old Shanghai* (Hong Kong: Oxford University Press, 1993), 26.

40   Byrna Goodman, 'Improvisations on a Semi-Colonial Theme, or, How to Read a Celebration of Transnational Urban Community', *Journal of Asian Studies* 59.4 (November 2000): 892.

41   'China – Foreign Concession'.

42   Goodman, 'Improvisations on a Semi-Colonial Theme', 892.

43   Bickers, *Empire Made Me*, 40.

44   Ibid. See also: Bickers, 'Shanghailanders', 161–211.

45   Lachlan Strahan, *Australia's China: Changing Perceptions from the 1930s to the 1990s* (Hong Kong: Cambridge University Press, 1996), 102.

46   Papers of Rex, Clarence and Madge Phillips, 1924–1946 Manuscripts Collection, National Library of Australia (NLA), MS 9942. See: Sophie Loy-Wilson, 'From Man of the British Empire to Proud Australian', *National Library News* (July 2008): 11–14.

47   Strahan, *Australia's China*, 106.

48   Ibid.

49   Ibid.

50 Sun Yat Sen once famously rejected the concept of 'semi-colonial' as failing to convey the true nature of China's relations with imperialist powers. See: Vivienne Shue, 'Sovereignty, Rule of Law, and Ideologies of Nation', *Journal of Asian Studies* 68.1 (February 2009): 102.

51 Ibid., 102. See, for example, Bryna Goodman, 'Improvisations on a Semi-Colonial Theme', 889–926.

52 Ruth Rogaski, *Hygienic Modernity: Meanings of Health and Disease in Treaty Port China* (Berkeley: University of California Press, 2004), 11.

53 Ibid., 11–12.

54 Fan-Ti Fan, 'Science in Cultural Borderlands: Methodological Reflections on the Study of Science, European Imperialism, and Cultural Encounter', *East Asian Science, Technology and Society: An International Journal* 1 (2007): 218. See also: Bryna Goodman and David S. Goodman, 'Introduction', in Bryna Goodman and David S. Goodman (eds.) *Twentieth-Century Colonialism and China: Localities, the Everyday and the World* (New York: Routledge, 2012), 1–23.

55 Ibid., 229.

56 'Australia' (澳州), *Global Half-Annual Journal* (*Huan Qiu Xun Kan*, 還球旬刊) 37 (1931): 37, SMA D2-0-2830-37.

57 For example see: H. Francessen, 'East for Trade: A Plea for a Wider Vision', *Rydge's Business Journal* (1 September 1932): 527–532.

58 Curthoys and (eds.) *Connected Worlds*, 8.

59 *Truth* (2 January 1916), 3.

60 Ibid., quoted in Max Kelly, *Faces of the Street: William Street Sydney 1916* (Sydney: Doak Press, 1982), 45.

61 Kevin Burley, *British Shipping and Australia 1920–1939* (London: Cambridge University Press, 1968), 56; John Bach, *A Maritime History of Australia* (Melbourne: Thomas Nelson Limited, 1976), 48.

62 'A&O Liners "Changte" and "Taiping"' postcard, *c*.1930, State Library of Victoria, H95.53/7.

63 Henry Champly, *The Road to Shanghai: White Slave Traffic in Asia*, translated from the French by Warre B. Wells (London: John Long, 1932), 165.

64 Ibid., 166.

65 'Girl's Million Dollar Job', *SMH*, 10 March 1927, 4.

66 Marilyn Lake, 'Chinese Colonists Assert Their Common Human Rights: Cosmopolitanism as Subject and Method in History', *Journal of World History* 21.3 (September 2010): 375–392; Kate Bagnall, 'Across the Threshold: White Women and Chinese Hawkers in the White Colonial Imaginary', *Hecate* 28.2 (2002): 9–29.

67 Raelene Frances, '"White Slaves" and White Australia: Prostitution and Australian Society', *Australian Feminist Studies* 19.44 (July 2004): 191.

68 Ibid., 190–193.

69 David Walker, *Anxious Nation: Australia and the Rise of Asia, 1850–1939* (St. Lucia: University of Queensland Press, 1999), 77.

70 'Commerce and Civilization' and 'The "China Trade" – Old and New', in Julius Klein, *Frontiers of Trade* (Washington, DC: The Century Co., 1929), 3–36, 289–304. See also: John Shepherd, *Australia's Interests and Policies in the Far East* (New York: Institute of Pacific Relations Inquiry Series, 1939); Nancy Windett, *Australia as a Producer and Trader 1920–1932* (Oxford: Oxford University Press, 1933).

71 Shepherd, *Australia's Interests*, 81. See also: *Australia and Industrial Development in Japan and China*, Bank of New South Wales Circular IV, March 1934.

72 G. E. Morrison to W. H. Donald, on board SS *Akira Maru*, 23 November 1917, 642–644.

73 'Australian Trade with China, the East and the Pacific Islands General', NAA CP703/5/23/A5131.

74　H. Gordon Bennett, 'The Function of Commercial Education', *Rydge's Business Journal* (1 February 1930): 103.

75　Ibid., 104.

76　Quoted in Strahan, *Australia's China*, 103; Frank Clune, *Sky High to Shanghai* (Sydney: Angus & Robertson, 1939). See also: Frank Clune, *Ashes of Hiroshima: A Post War Trip to China and Japan* (Sydney: Angus & Robertson, 1992), 234–235, 247.

77　Speech by the Right Hon. J. G. Latham, CMG, KC, on the Australian Eastern Mission Report, Parliamentary Debates, 6 July 1934, 'Goodwill Trade Mission Report', NAA A981 FAR 5 PART 16.

78　Ibid.

79　Ibid.

80　J. H. C. Sleeman, *White China: An Austral-Asian Sensation* (Sydney: self-published, 1933), 303. See also: Sophie Loy-Wilson 'Peanuts and Publicists: "Letting Australian Friends Know the Chinese Side of the Story" in Interwar Sydney', *History Australia* 6.1 (April 2009): 1–20.

81　Sleeman, *White China.* 235.

82　Antonia Finnane, *Far from Where? Jewish Journeys from Shanghai to Australia* (Carlton: University of Melbourne Press, 1999), 37.

83　Ibid., 37.

84　Ibid., 58.

85　Bickers, 'Shanghailanders', 158.

86　Robert Bickers and Jeffrey N. Wasserstrom, 'Shanghai "Dogs and Chinese Not Admitted" Sign: Legend, History and Contemporary Symbol', *China Quarterly* (1995): 1.

87　Antonia Finnane, *Far from Where?*, 37.

88　Bickers and Wasserstrom, 'Shanghai "Dogs and Chinese Not Admitted" Sign'.

89　Karl Gerth, *China Made: Consumer Culture and the Creation of the Nation* (Cambridge, MA: Harvard University Press, 2004), 2–3.

90　Ibid., 5.

91　Ibid., 3.

92　Ibid., 7.

93　Ibid., 40; Rogaski, *Hygienic Modernity*, 11, 302.

94　Frederica Ferlanti, 'The New Life Movement in Jiangxi Province 1934–1938', *Modern Asian Studies* 44.5 (2010): 963.

95　Mark S. Eykholt, 'Resistance to Opium as a Social Evil in Wartime China', in Timothy Brook and Bob Tadashi Wakabayashi (eds.) *Opium Regimes: China, Britain and Japan 1839–1952* (Berkeley: University of California Press, 2000), 363–364.

96　Carlton Benson, 'Consumers Are Also Soldiers: Subversive Songs from Nanjing Road during the New Life Movement', in Sherman Cochran (ed.) *Inventing Nanjing Road: Commercial Culture in Shanghai, 1900–1945* (Ithaca, NY: Cornell East Asian Studies, 1999), 90–132.

97　Bennett, 'The Function of Commercial Education', 103.

98　J. R. Hinterland, 'The Traveling-Representative and His Duties: Catering for Trade in the East', *Rydge's Business Journal* (July 1931): 465. See also: J. R. Hinterland, 'Why Does Australia Not Get Her Share of the Eastern Trade?', *Rydge's Business Journal* (June 1931): 371–373.

99　Philippa Levine, 'Modernity, Medicine and Colonialism: The Contagious Diseases Ordinance in Hong Kong and the Straights Settlement', in Antoinette Burton (ed.) *Gender, Sexuality and Colonial Modernities* (London: Routledge, 1999), 44.

4 Class and Commerce in Australian Expatriate Communities

The Chinese people are our near neighbours in the Pacific. Shanghai is 2,000 miles nearer to Sydney than is San Francisco. China's millions can be more important to Australia than America's millions. Shanghai is one of the five largest ports in the world.[1]

E. V. Elliot, Federal Secretary, Australian Seamen's Union, 4 September 1946

It is impossible to know if the optimistic visions of commercial triumph espoused by some Australians towards the Eastern markets had in any way influenced the decision of one Allan Willoughby Raymond to migrate from Australia to Shanghai in search of work. Born in Melbourne on 27 February 1909, Raymond's Shanghai Municipal Police (SMP) file dated his arrival in Shanghai to 1929, but precisely when and how he arrived there is unclear.[2] In the early 1930s he lived in a boarding house near Bubbling Well Road in Shanghai, where he rented a room with an Australian piano player named Harry Kerry, 46, who was mostly unemployed but worked in various local bands playing in 'cabarets, cafes etc.'.[3] In 1930 Kerry already had a police file for drunken behaviour and non-payment of debts. 'He indulges in alcoholic bouts from time to time and is quite unfit for work on these occasions', police noted in Kerry's surveillance file. 'He is now unwanted for bands and can only get employment as a solo player.'[4] The boarding house in which Kerry and Raymond lived enjoyed a poor reputation among both local Chinese and European residents. SMP officers called the Kinvig Boarding House at 30 Weihaiwei Road '[a] disgraceful, unsanitary institution and a hotbed of gambling and Bolshevism'.[5] Its owner, Marion Maud Kinvig, was born in Sydney on 24 December 1878. She came to the attention of the SMP after 'attempting to conduct the premises as a gambling establishment'.[6] SMP officers noted her possession of a British passport issued at Batavia on 15 February 1928 and her arrival in Shanghai from Java in February 1930.[7] Marion Kinvig was just one of many Australians identified by police constables during the SMP crackdown on gambling in 1929.[8]

Shanghai operated on the chit system, under which Europeans could get credit in stores and restaurants, provided that they settled up on the first of each month. Raymond lost his job again and ran up debts that he was unable to repay. In an effort to get square he visited the city's pony racing track and the Canidrome greyhound track in Frenchtown. One of the city's biggest gamblers was fellow Australian Dr Bill O'Hara, but whereas O'Hara was a frequent winner, Raymond invariably lost. As his financial problems increased, he wrote a number of dishonoured cheques to business associates and his name was 'posted' at the Shanghai Race Club for unpaid debts.

Shunned by Europeans for his dishonesty – and possibly because of his Eurasian appearance – Raymond socialised with the less-principled members of Shanghai's racing fraternity. 'His association with low Chinese women, Japs and Germans made him an object of loathing among reputable Britishers in Shanghai', the Sydney branch of the Australian Security Service reported in 1943. Raymond thought that this attitude was applied to Australians in general. In a post-war statement he wrote:

> During the years I spent in the East I became conscious that the general attitude on behalf of the Britishers here towards Australians was one of superiority and condescension. I also observed that we had little direct communication with China and other countries here and even had to negotiate drafts on Australian banks through London. I came to the conclusion that direct contact was urgently needed if we were to derive the greatest benefit from our geographical location near the Orient.[9]

The presence of these Australians and the ways in which they lived could make the British-dominated administration's hold over Shanghai's International Settlement seem increasingly fragile. Australians had to tailor their poverty to Shanghai's high costs, often transgressing the norms of the broader white community: marrying or cohabiting with Asian, Eurasian or Russian women; living in Chinese housing; and working with or for Chinese. In contrast to British India, the Shanghai Municipal Council was ill equipped to deal with problem populations of whites. Distressed British subjects could be shipped home, criminals could be deported to Hong Kong after serving their time, and dismissed policemen could be refused their superannuation unless they took it back to Britain. However, poverty and destitution could not be hidden.[10] A series of interviews conducted by Antonia Finnane with members of the Shanghai Jewish community evacuated to Australia during the Second World War documents the conditions experienced by some Australians in the city's boarding houses. These were often crowded – due in the first instance to the poverty of the inhabitants. 'On the ground you would find dead babies wrapped in these bamboo mats', Hilda Weininger remembered: 'There were beggars without limbs. For me it was a terrible experience.'[11] Throughout the 1920s and 1930s Shanghai had one of the highest rates of exposed street corpses in the world. Christian Henriot's research on the Shanghai Municipal Council's morgue files found that over 5,000 bodies per month were picked up off Shanghai streets in the early 1930s. 'These figures and these numbers show that there was almost no way for an ordinary Shanghai resident during these years to escape the view of dead children and adults lying in the streets or alleyways.'[12] Kitty Brodtmann's neighbours were a Chinese family of eight, all living in one room. Paul Wagenberg had a Chinese friend who worked in a rice shop, and whose job it was to stand behind the bars protecting the front of the shop by poking people away with a stick so that only one customer was served at a time. In return for this service he was allowed to sleep on the shop counter at night, but his mother and siblings all slept on the street.[13] Australian horse trader Rex Phillips did not tell his family in Melbourne about his living conditions until they had improved: 'I am much more happy these days because I have got a district, and the best District in Shanghai at that, namely:– Bubbling Well. It's a clean district with good class work.'[14] The combination of war in Europe and the Great Depression meant that many whites in Shanghai began to live in similar urban conditions to the Chinese majority, complicating the class and labour dynamics of the city. The Kinvig boarding house was no exception and stood shoulder-to-shoulder with Chinese slum districts.[15] One of the reasons SMP officers could distinguish Australians from other whites was because Australians congregated with other Australians in well-known boarding houses such as the Kinvig residence. Boarding-house living solidified an association between Australian urban dwellers in Shanghai and criminal activity.

Allan Raymond's early attempts at trade met with failure. He tried to sell imported Australian goods to Chinese local shops but this business never succeeded. We can only speculate as to why this was. Significant anti-imperialist boycotts of British goods occurred in Shanghai in 1931. Karl Gerth argues that these boycotts were the most visible – and the most violent – manifestation of anti-foreigner sentiment in China at the time.[16] Li Jianhong, a participant in the boycotts, described his feelings in a National Products Movement pamphlet in 1925: 'Chinese history is replete with humiliations at the hands of foreigners . . . indeed, in commercial affairs, not a day passes without the continuation of evil hegemonic policies directed against China.'[17] Shopkeepers were urged to tell customers who asked for imported products: 'I'm sorry, we don't have foreign products, we only have national products.'[18] The 1930s was not, therefore, an ideal time to begin selling Australian goods in China. 'There is not a house in Asia that is sympathetic to Australian produce', declared trader J. B. Suttor, 'Australia has an awful name in China . . . In Shanghai the Australia trade is shrinking.'[19]

Australia journalist J. H. C. Sleeman, who worked closely with Sydney's Chinese community, joined the chorus of criticism of Australia's efforts in the China market in his book *White China* in 1933: 'In China, Australian products are condemned on account of unattractive labels . . . Australian exporters ignore suggestions regarding size and shape of tins and style of labels made by merchants in the East.'[20] Citing the work of Queensland academic and sinologist A. C. V. Melbourne, whose influential 'Report on Australian Intercourse with Japan and China' was widely read in 1932, Sleeman wrote: 'Dr. Melbourne pointed out that we lost our biscuit trade in the East because we refused to pack them in the way desired by Orientals.'[21] Further, he cited the complaints of W. Ranger, Manager of the Committee of Fruit Marketing, who in 1930 reported that 'the oranges we export to Shanghai were too sour, skin too thick, abnormal number of seeds, tough pulp and little juice. Traders had to sell at less than cost price to clear the line. We have not made any effort to remedy these very valid grievances.'[22]

Files in the National Archives of Australia, containing photographs of Australian goods being readied for export to China and Japan, are informative.[23] Australian dried fruit was arranged to look like the various symbols of the British monarchy or in a Union Jack formation. Fruit tins were labelled 'White Peaches of Empire' and also displayed the Union Jack. Taking their cue from the iconography popular at empire-wide industrial exhibitions, these labels extended the theatrical pageantry of empire into a transcolonial consumer culture. The didactics of this theatre were about power, and the ways in which the power of empire 'could reach out over distance, can have permanence even without presence', as when 'the Tamil coolie quenches his thirst with an emptied British milk tin, or the naked piccaninni clutches a milk bottle made in Leeds'.[24] In this way, the labels of Australian-made products were potentially offensive to Chinese customers and used symbols increasingly associated with the very imperialist processes that Chinese consumers were in the process of boycotting.

Commercial relationships between salesmen such as Allan Raymond and Chinese traders were structured on various levels by economic rituals that concealed the operation of colonial power behind the fiction of an exchange between equals. Under the conditions of colonial governance in China, commercial

Figure 4.1 Australian dried fruit 'sample', 'Advertising, Subsidies to Industries for Advertising', NAA A2489/1/1920/3344.

encounters between whites and Chinese were never simple financial transactions. By the 1930s for many Chinese these exchanges symbolised their humiliation under imperial rule. While established European, Japanese and American traders may have been aware of these dynamics, newly arrived Australian traders were not. When Australians moved to Shanghai, they brought with them a dense set of derogatory cultural stereotypes about China dating back to the gold rushes of the 1860s and perhaps earlier. As Marilyn Lake and many others have argued, the racism provoked in such settler societies as Australia by Chinese migration was virulent, resulting not only in restrictions on Chinese immigration to Australia, but also in the proliferation of anti-Chinese cultural tropes and ways of thinking.[25] In some ways, a large part of identifying as an Australian nationalist was synonymous with identifying as anti-Chinese. So we can perhaps assume that salesmen like Allan Raymond would likely have presumed their superiority over local Chinese in ways unhelpful to any business venture.

After Allan Raymond's import and export business failed, he sought out increasingly menial forms of employment.[26] But manual work was also hard to find. Shanghai had a large unskilled labour force. It was rare for Europeans to be able to compete successfully with the poorly paid Chinese in the Shanghai labour market. Jewish refugee Paul Wagenberg was shocked to see one young man: 'a white man – white was a big thing of course as compared to the Chinese: everybody was racist – and he was going round and round pulling a stone mill all day long, grinding coal into dust from which later briquettes were made'.[27] Unable to find work in European companies, Raymond sought employment in Chinese businesses. From 1932 to 1935 he was employed by Chinese businessman Jacob Wong of the Shanghai Marble Co. on Jin Kiang Road as a foreign salesman and correspondent.

In 1935 Wong moved his business to 437 Singapore Road but dispensed with Raymond's services. However, he allowed him to use the address and Raymond established a firm known as the Metropolitan Marble Co. on the premises.

> Raymond acted in the capacity of broker and took orders and commissions for stone work some of which he failed to fill although receiving the money in advance. By 1937 Raymond's business was practically non-existent and he had accumulated a number of debts including unpaid chits at the Shanghai Race Club where he was a member and ardent race follower.[28]

Police wrote of his

> spendthrift nature and his fondness for luxuries, insofar as whenever he brought off a good business deal he would squander the money on gambling and pleasure seeking. In this respect there have been occasions when his client's money became indistinguishable from his own.[29]

He went to Wusieh, where he took over the job of protecting a Chinese factory. He was next heard of in Hong Kong, 'where after an incident connected with the running of a pony at the Macau Races which was witnessed by the Stewards of the Hong Kong Jockey Club, Raymond was warned off the Course at Hong Kong'.[30] He subsequently returned to Shanghai, where he was homeless for a time before applying for funds at the local office of the ANZAC Relief Society.

SMP biographies and surveillance files wrote the lives of Australians in Shanghai into a 'tragic narrative' or a 'narrative of decline'. Reports on Australians were peppered with a logic that assumed the predictability of their business failure, financial distress and moral corruption once immersed in treaty port life. These narratives tell us more about British attitudes to the category 'Australian' between the wars than they do about the lived reality of Australians in Shanghai. For the various authors of Allan Raymond's surveillance file, 'Australians had a penchant for criminality'.[31] Australians were often an embarrassment for SMP constables, 'inevitably losing' when gambling or boxing or 'predictably drunk' and out of work.[32] As their lives unfold in SMP files, Australians are presented as out of place in Shanghai, and as symbols of the weakening of white power in the East. Such anxieties were also reflected at higher levels, for example in the correspondence between the Australian government and the British government over a possible ban on Australians entering Shanghai in the 1930s.[33]

Raymond was one of many Australians to experience downward social mobility after his arrival in Shanghai. Uschi Hirche remembered unemployed Europeans patronising her father's tailor shop on Hongkew: 'The immigrants were very poor. If they had a suit that got shiny, they couldn't afford to buy a new suit. They had to reverse it, inside out. And we always said, "I'm sorry" when they came back with the suit: "That hasn't got a third side. That's the end of the suit." '[34] SMP officials noted a worrying propensity among Australians to slide into criminality. Jack Boyle (alias Nick Boyle), a native of Newcastle, 'sponges on his friends for support and sometimes takes part in boxing matches, invariably losing', wrote DSI Laurier in a Special Branch report in 1937.[35] After his import–export business went bust, Boyle worked on the Shanghai and Hongkew wharf for a time. However, he was discharged from this position 'owing to malfeasance'.[36] Police reports show he was brought to Shanghai's Central Police Station for being drunk and, while there overnight, kicked through a portion of the wire netting of the detention cell. Later, at the insistence of the ANZAC Relief Society, he was sent to Hong Kong for the purpose of joining the Royal Navy but appeared before the naval authorities there in such a drunken state that he had to be sent away. 'Boyle is a waster and habitual drunkard and practically unemployable', wrote DSI Laurier. 'He has no fixed abode at present and is believed to be sleeping out, or in cheap Chinese lodging houses . . . During his stay in Shanghai he was associated with the worst element.'[37]

By 1932 the 'problem' of Australians in Shanghai was the subject of correspondence between British and Australian authorities. The British government hoped to stem the tide of Australians into the city by requesting the Australian authorities to issue an official warning. It was not only that Australians were becoming increasingly burdensome on the police and consular bureaucracies; as recipients of white privilege, they also threatened to undermine its power.

Unemployed Australians in the city exposed some of the contradictions inherent in imperial rule. Unlike resident Chinese, Australians could lay claim to some of the highest institutional rights to mobility and commerce that the city had to offer. Using their passports, they could enter any of the city's European concessions freely and could trade at a lower tax rate than Chinese locals and stateless Europeans. Eddie Welham, who moved to Melbourne from Shanghai's Hongkew Jewish ghetto in 1941, remembered the strange case of Eddie Moyhing, whom he met in a Japanese prisoner-of-war camp for British subjects in Shanghai after the Japanese invasion in 1939.

> Eddie Moyhing, who is Chinese, absolutely pure Chinese. So you say to yourself, how come he's in a British camp? It was because his father was born in Australia: he might have been a descendant of the gold miners. His father being born in Australia, he had an Australian passport. In those days Australians held British passports.[38]

The flow of Australians into Shanghai in the 1930s posed significant challenges for the imperial authorities – at a time when mobility within empire, and mobility between 'white man's country' and other colonial sites, were contested issues. How to manage working-class Australians who washed up in the world of treaty port China was a complex matter.

The case of Jack Edward Ivers illustrates this broader dilemma. Ivers was born in the small settlement of St Arnaud Victoria in 1905. He arrived in Shanghai from Sydney in about September 1926 and soon earned for himself the reputation 'of being an absolute waster'.[39] He was also suspected 'of being a pimp'.[40] After his import and export business went badly, he couldn't obtain any regular employment and, in March 1927, applied at the local office of the ANZAC Relief Society for assistance. Arrangements were made to send him back to Australia and a passage was booked for him to Hong Kong on the S *Rwaltapindi*; however, he failed to embark when the vessel sailed.[41] Ivers then began a relationship with a Russian prostitute named Pelagine Kovenko. He lived with her for a period of time, but on 4 August 1927 the couple argued. Four soldiers intervened and Ivers was evicted from the premises. He was later arrested on a British Supreme Court warrant and charged with five cases of obtaining money by fraud and false pretences. He was found guilty and sentenced to be kept in custody until he was put on board a vessel bound for Australia.

However, he did not remain away from Shanghai for long:

> On 26 January 1928 he was arrested on North Szechuen Road for carrying unlicensed firearms. He appeared before the British Court on 27 January 1928 and was sentenced to one month's imprisonment with hard labor, the pistol and immunities found in his possession to be confiscated by the SMP. Upon his release from prison Ivers again became associated with Mrs. Pelagine L Kovenko, and as he was unemployed he lived on money supplied to him by her. Mrs. Kovenko at that time was an inmate of a brothel

at 2 Fearson Road. In October 1927 she became one of the licensees of the premises but did not change her mode of living. She was trying to marry Ivers hoping that by doing so she would be able to enter Australia with him.

During June 1928 Ivers and Mrs. Kovenko made applications to marry at the British Consulate General in Shanghai and went through a form of marriage some time later. Ivers obtained one or two minor jobs but again applied to the ANZAC Society for assistance. He was sent to the 'Crystal Hotel' 37 Seward Rd where he resided for a period at the expense of the association. In Sept 1928 Ivers who has recently registered himself at the British Consulate General in Shanghai applied there for a passport for himself and his wife. A report of the characters and activities of Ivers and his wife was sent to the British Consulate General by the SMP and on the strength of this report a passport was refused Mrs. Ivers. Ivers obtained passport on Sept 24 1928 with a paragraph inserted by the Acting Consul General that it should not be made valid for the British Empire. British authorities were clear that they did not want 'this type of person' to be in possession of British citizenship. A memo requesting that Ivers and his wife were to be stopped from entering the British Empire was forwarded to the HM Minister in Peiking. Before the circular had time to take effect, however, Ivers applied for a passport for himself and his wife at Mukden and Harbin and was granted passports in Harbin on 12 October 1928 for himself and his wife. Ivers returned to Shanghai after this and his wife later returned to the USSR.[42]

In 1934 evidence was produced in Shanghai showing that at the time that Pelagine Kovenko got married to Ivers she was already married, thus making her marriage to Ivers bigamous. On the strength of this, the British authorities in Shanghai considered the marriage nullified and Mrs Kovenko immediately lost her British nationality and any rights and privileges she may have enjoyed as the wife of a British subject. In August 1934 Ivers applied to the Salvation Army in Shanghai for assistance, stating that he had been discharged from the Customs Service for excessive drinking. He received assistance from the Salvation Army authorities and in September 1934 obtained employment with Messrs Mollers Ltd. He stopped working for this company in May 1935. His movements for the next year or two are rather obscure, until on 13 July 1937 he obtained a position as Second Officer with Butterfield & Swire Ltd, but was discharged for excessive drinking on 5 July 1938. He again applied to the Relief Society for assistance in February 1939.[43]

Fears of anti-British and communist activism in the 1930s meant closer surveillance of those suspected of seditious activities, with the formation of an Australian section in the Criminal Investigation Department of the SMP in the 1930s. Ivers's file was produced in part by this section. The British shared intelligence about Australians across imperial networks that spanned the empire. Records were kept of Australians leaving Shanghai, and detailed biographies were compiled on the background of those who applied to work for the SMP. Webs of empire were also evident in the consular network, which shaped concern over events such as Mrs Johnson's conviction for narcotic manufacture and sale in 1934.

Much was made in Ivers's file about his relationship with Mrs Kovenko and how, for long periods of time, he lived off her income. Descriptions of Australians as childlike and dependent on wives, mothers, prostitutes or local women proliferated in SMP files. Concern over a perceived deficiency in Australian masculinity and the corruption of this masculinity once in the Far East was a hallmark of such biographies.[44] In 1938 the biography of one Sidney Frank Hearne was circulated between British consulates in Shanghai and Hong Kong.[45] Hearne, an Australian, was born in Kobe, Japan, where his father had been a hotel manager. His childhood was partly spent in China, before he travelled to Australia and served in the Australian military forces. 'Accompanied by his mother he travelled from Sydney to Shanghai on the SS *Nellore*, arriving on 10 October 1938. He is described by a fellow passenger as completely under his mother's influence.'[46] Hearne's conversation 'indicated that his mentality is more like that of a child than a young man'.[47] On the same day he arrived Hearne applied for a position on the Shanghai Municipal Gaol staff ('with the help of his mother') and was given the usual educational test but failed to qualify, 'his spelling and grammar being very poor etc.'.[48] Hearne's relationship with his mother and Ivers's with Mrs Kovenko were here reflective of a broader problem: the dependence of some Australians on charity and welfare while in Shanghai and the strain that they placed on the British imperial administration.

By taking menial jobs and engaging in criminal enterprise, Australians like Ivers and Hearne troubled colonial hierarchies that linked poverty and squalor with native populations and wealth and success with resident white populations, especially Anglo-Saxon ones. Concurrently, the circulation of Australian products carrying empire iconography solidified the link between Australians and empire building. For Henry Champly, the spectacle of Australian criminality in Shanghai's cabaret bars was of serious concern. He wrote of establishments with 'Queen Ann chairs and red carpets' where 'yellow men with three chins' mixed with Australian prostitutes: 'Yes, indeed, those great world-teachers of virtue, the Anglo-Saxons of every sect, have taught the little Chinese coolies that Australian women – are the most debauched women on the earth.'[49] At a time of increasing anti-foreign and anti-imperial sentiment in China, Australian behaviour in Shanghai threatened to upset the foundations of British claims to sovereignty: urban improvement schemes, law and order and morality. As Champly wrote in *The Road to Shanghai* in 1932: 'If the Whites, in colonial countries, could show themselves superior to all carnal and moral failings, then it would be easy enough for them to correct the abuses and outrages of the native.'[50]

By directly requesting that Australians stop moving to Shanghai for work, British authorities signalled their anxieties over the impact of Australians on 'white prestige' in the city. Australian bureaucrats with interests in the Eastern markets were similarly concerned by the reports from the SMP about Australians in Shanghai, as well as rising 'anti-white' sentiment in China more generally. Sir Herbert Gepp, President of the Australian Board of Trade and Chairman of the Australian Development and Migration Commission, requested information on the treaty port system from the British authorities.[51] He wrote to Sir Austen

Chamberlain enquiring about 'Article II of the Treaty of Nanking – for [Australian] Trading Purposes'.[52] He was told that:

> The actual position in regard to foreign settlements in China does not seem to be clearly understood in Great Britain. Only a few months ago a prominent politician, speaking in the House of Commons, expressed the opinion that it was not surprising that there was agitation in China 'when the external powers took forty-nine Chinese cities giving them no share in the government of these cities'.[53]

By 1929 the problem of Chinese anti-imperialism in the treaty ports led the Shanghai Municipal Council to invite Judge Feetham of the South African Supreme Court to come and 'study the seeming paradox of a large group of Chinese residing on Chinese soil under foreign government'.[54] In light of the Feetham report, the case of Tsing dao (Qingdao) attracted considerable attention in Britain and China. Qingdao had been placed under German control in 1897 and was considered 'a model city' – a testament to the virtues of European governance in China.[55] After the city was restored to the Chinese in 1922, British authorities claimed, it had fallen into ruin.

> Not only have the local Chinese authorities [in Qingdao] since violated every undertaking into which they entered in respect of foreign participation in the municipal administration, but they have since been doing their best to ruin the port.[56]

The British criticised the Chinese for cutting down £30,000 worth of trees, neglecting to dredge the wharves and harbours, and allowing thick deposits of dirt and coal dust to cover the sidewalks and streets. Qingdao today, they concluded, 'is rapidly deteriorating and this would be the fate of any foreign concessions or Settlements which might be given back to the Chinese'.[57] In this way, the British countered Chinese anticolonialism through examples taken from the urban environment, which, they believed, demonstrated a British ability to administer public space and public behaviour in a 'civilised' and 'orderly way'.

At the same time anti-imperialist nationalists in China demanded foreign concessions be returned to Chinese administration. 'Foreigners are not satisfied each day unless they have extracted more concessions from China', wrote Li Jian Hong in 1925.[58] A series of reports prepared in 1923 by American consulates across China observed the links between foreign humiliations of China and a growing sense of anti-imperialism.[59] A report from Ji'nan, the provincial capital of Shandong, concluded, for instance, that aggression on the part of foreigners 'arouses feelings of intense antagonism and opposition and a sense of injustice, humiliation and degradation suffered at foreign hands'.[60] The report also observed changing attitudes among children, who now brazenly called foreigners 'foreign devils' and were not 'rebuked or checked by their elders'.[61] On the eve of a boycott these reports also noted that this environment was undermining the ability of foreigners to do business in China.[62] Travelling through the Chinese countryside in the early 1920s, Australian saleswoman Beatrice Thompson confirmed these reports in her letters to the Australian authorities. She had twice been captured by local Chinese when marketing 'perfumery and cosmetics' in outlying villages.[63]

Arguments countering Chinese anticolonialism and justifying Britain's imperial presence in China on the basis of urban development and civility were reflected in the letters written home by Australians in Shanghai and in popular literature. 'The real China is nowhere like [the treaty ports]', wrote Champly in *The Road to Shanghai*. 'It is drab, plain and poor. I know of only one place in Asia which achieves the cleanliness, the style, and the gaiety of that pseudo-China of the cinema. It is in English territory.'[64] Horse trader Rex Phillips told his family in Melbourne: 'The British BUILT Shanghai and the Chinese want to take it off the British.'[65] He responded strongly to the views of Chinese Australian businessman Louey Pang, who had advocated Shanghai's return to China in the Australian press:

> That cutting about Louey Pang which you sent made me want to have five minutes with Louey. He says that China is now a MODERN country, and able to govern herself etc. etc. Last year when Louey was in Shanghai he stayed at a big Chinese owned and managed hotel, Wing On's by name. After stopping there a few days he moved to a foreign owned and managed hotel, The Palace by name, and when I asked him why he moved he said, 'Oh the Chinese are too dirty for words, besides they make such a hell of a din.' Now dear Louey thinks so much of the 'modernised' China which he spouts about from Australia, the best example he could set is to come and live in Chinese territory. It's just this Louey Pang is just an ordinary example of the vast majority of Chinese, a lying, oily, twister. PS Wing On's is considered the best Chinese Hotel in Shanghai.[66]

Central to such arguments was not only Britain's architectural and institutional presence in treaty ports like Shanghai but also the behaviour of Britons – and, by extension, Australian Britons – in these spaces. Invasion and dispossession in settler societies had long been justified on the basis that indigenous populations did not use the land productively. Rightful occupation of the land was connected to perceptions of 'development' and progress. Arguments about Chinese misuse of Shanghai's resources figured native Chinese as dependent on Europeans for their living standards, health and hygiene, and urban improvement schemes. The category of 'Australian' complicated such colonial binaries. If Europeans were the authority on civilised settlement, why were white Australians abandoning their homes in Australia and – in an inversion of the colonial order of things – travelling to China for work? And why, once in China, were they so patently unproductive and unsuccessful in their labours? In order to fully explicate the weight of these contradictions in 1930s Shanghai, we need to consult interwar Chinese attitudes towards 'Australia'.

Reports about Australia appeared frequently in the Chinese press in the 1920s and 1930s. In 1928 the *Eastern Magazine*, or *Dongfang Zhouzhi* (東方周知), ran a feature article tracing Australia's history since British colonisation.[67] Australia was a country sustained on 'the agriculture of sheep', or *Mu yangye* (牧羊葉), the article read, and was a 'British colony' populated by 'nothing more than prisoners'.[68] Australia had run free elections since Federation in 1901 but Britain still 'dictated policy'.[69] Inherited criminality was a common theme in this Chinese press coverage of Australia. Chinese responses to Australia in such publications as this laid bare the absurdities of European claims to civilised attributes based on race. They juxtaposed the superior attitudes of the British in China with the 'peasant ways' of 'Australian prisoners'. Here was a view of Australians through Chinese eyes that bordered on the satirical. Australia was a 'retrograde nation', or *tuihua minzu*, and Australian nationals lacked *guanzhan* or 'civility'.[70]

These articles were published in the shadow of debates over Australian prejudice towards Chinese immigrants. The issue dominating Chinese coverage of Australia from the 1920s on was Australia's immigration restriction legislation. The Immigration Restriction Act 1901 confirmed and extended a number of policies and laws existing in the pre-Federation Australian colonies (see Introduction). Inherent in these policies was the belief that Australia was rightfully a 'white man's country'; the Act was to keep 'aboriginal natives of Asia, Africa and the Pacific' out.[71] In 1934 the *Eastern Magazine* (東方周知) published an article entitled 'Australia as a Coloniser', which was highly critical of the policy, while in 1933 the *Global Half-Annual Journal*, or *Huan Qiu Xun Kan* (還球旬刊), criticised the 'aggressive racial prejudice of Australia's immigration restriction laws'.[72] Australians, the journal argued, were willing to go to violent lengths 'in order to maintain the purity of the race, unity of their civilization and of White Australia'.[73] Chinese diplomats wanting to travel to Australia were often 'refused passports'.[74] The result of the White Australia Policy, the article argued, was a lack of trade with Asia and, therefore, a slow rate of economic development in Australia coupled with high unemployment.[75] 'They think we are all opium users', complained a Chinese soccer player who had travelled to Australia as part of a specially arranged tour in 1928; 'our rank in their society is very low'.[76] Australian race prejudice towards the Chinese, the soccer player argued, forced Chinese in Australia to live a degraded existence. Encountering local Chinese had been a 'humiliating' experience. 'The most painful thing is that the Chinese Australians do not have knowledge. They are lower class Cantonese.'[77] His opinion echoed complaints made more than a decade earlier by the Chinese consul general in Australia in a letter to G. E. Morrison in 1914:

As we can only get a certain class of Cantonese to come out here we can only hope to get a certain type of treatment. However there is at least one most unfair and unjust law existing that is some Chinese who are allowed to stay and do business here are denied the facility to bring their family out even for a visit from time to time, the result could not be beneficial to any party. As I am quite powerless in this direction, I sincerely hope that on your next visit to your Fatherland you will do your best to adjust this inhumane regulation.[78]

Thus, Chinese attitudes to Australians in the 1920s and 1930s – and, for our purposes, Australians in Shanghai – were filtered through a Chinese knowledge of Australian history as well as elite Chinese perceptions of provincial Cantonese migrants.

Chinese resentment over the White Australia Policy was brought to the attention of Australian trade officials in 1931, when Chinese newspapers in Shanghai published a translation of an article from the Australian newspaper *Smith's Weekly* entitled 'Hard for a Brisbane Girl to Work'.[79] Based on the author's visits to a number of department stores in Brisbane, the article argued that Australian unemployment was caused by Asian imports: 'Our girls want work and are not likely to get it if the vogue of importing ready-made frocks from Shanghai is persisted in.'[80] While Australian women languished in poverty, *Smith's Weekly* argued, Chinese merchants were growing rich by importing goods into Australia: 'The unemployed Brisbane girl has the satisfaction of knowing that Slit Eye in Shanghai is getting a nice, comfortable living by exporting frocks to Queensland if that is any consolation.'[81] The author of the article claimed to have observed customs procedures on Brisbane wharves and discovered that no precautions were taken with regard to disease in dresses brought in from China. But since the introduction of second-hand clothing from China was 'strictly prohibited . . . this was an admission that disease might lurk in Oriental imports. Brushes of all kinds are not allowed in.'[82] Upon visiting Brisbane's department stores, the author was told by salesgirls that gowns come in regularly from Shanghai and were simply unpacked and sold, despite 'being handled by eastern factory workers'.[83] '[Money] is spent in giving a living to Misses Ah Chum and Low How in Shanghai, but the girls who spend what little money they have in Brisbane stores are cut out from that much work.'[84] Once translated, 'Hard for a Brisbane Girl to Work' circulated widely in Shanghai. Australian salesman Mr V. J. Palstra, a resident of Shanghai, wrote to the Australian government in protest: 'It is a matter of regret that such an article should be published.'[85] Palstra warned of a general boycott of Australian goods in China if the government did not intervene:

> Unless we manage to retain the goodwill of the Chinese there is not a hope of us securing for Australia her rightful position in this market. It is quite within the realms of possibility that the incident I have just detailed to you might have a serious effect on Australian trade in this country. In the past boycotts have been started on account of lesser happenings. If the Chinese chamber of commerce get hold of the facts for instance there would be an outcry against things Australian. The Chinese resent very strongly any suggestion of inferiority.[86]

The factory in question, Palstra pointed out, was run by Chinese but *staffed* by Australians. Dr N. H. Kung, Minister of Commerce and Industry in the Chinese

Nationalist government, asked his officials at the *Waichiaopu* (Foreign Office) to take the matter up through the Chinese consul general of Australia. The affair occurred in the context of broader resentment in China over the White Australia Policy. In November of the same year the Australian prime minister, James Scullin, was questioned on the subject in the House of Representatives. Mr Green, a wheat farmer, informed the prime minister that Chinese workers were refusing to unload Australian flour on Chinese wharves, part of a general boycott of Australian goods:

> Has the Prime Minister seen a newspaper report that because of the discrim-ination against Chinese goods by the Commonwealth retaliatory measures against imports from Australia are being taken by the Government of the Chinese Republic? If so what steps does the Commonwealth government propose to take? There is more than a threatened boycott of Australian goods; Chinese traders are refusing to handle them. If the position in the East does not improve our natural market will be closed against us. It is within our power to remove the conditions to which China objects. £1,000 of Australian wheat rot on the wharfs of Shanghai![87]

We can read this event as part of an extended commercial encounter between Chinese workers and consumers and Australian traders and government officials. Within the encounter, Australian attitudes towards Chinese products (in the first instance, dresses from Shanghai) were conflated with Australian race prejudice more generally. Talk of diseased dresses and brushes on the bodies of Australian women made a commercial relationship into a racialised and sexualised relationship, whereby using Chinese products was akin to being 'touched' or 'infected' by a Chinese factory worker. In this way, *Smith's Weekly* drew upon common tropes surrounding the sexual exploitation of white women, or 'White Slaves', by 'Yellow Men' or, as Henry Champly put it: 'The initiation of the coloured people into the extraordinary charm of the White Venus.'[88]

The encounter was complicated by the circulation of the *Smith's Weekly* article among Chinese readers in Shanghai who were probably aware of the growing problem of Australian criminality in Chinese treaty ports. At moments like these, Australia's encounter with Asia must be viewed from the bottom up – the lives of men like Jack Ivers and Allan Raymond must be made to speak to larger historical problems. Their presence in Shanghai exposed the opera-tion of colonial power in ways especially provocative to local Chinese. First, their ability to come to Shanghai demonstrated an ease of mobility that was off limits to native Chinese, not only within the empire but also within their own city and country. Second, their behaviour exposed the double standard of the British justice system as it operated in Chinese treaty ports – Australian opium smugglers were allowed to return home, while Chinese caught in possession of the drug were liable to be handed over to Chinese authorities and executed. Finally, while Chinese products were represented as inferior and diseased in Australian popular newspapers, Australian products were sold to Chinese consumers in packaging that celebrated the very 'White Australia' that Chinese citizens were banned from entering. By refusing to unload Australian wheat on Shanghai's wharves, Chinese workers gestured to the colonial paradox of trading with an Asian nation, on the one hand, while simultaneously excluding its citizens, on the other.

***

In 1894, in the pages of the *Launceston Examiner*, R. H. Maeburn painted a picture of Asia as a salesman's dreamland for white colonists:

> I know for a fact that an enormous trade is done with the native races of Southern Asia in European goods . . . The growing population of those cattle-less countries are now reared on milk procured from cows fed on Swiss pastures. The Burmese mother quiets the family hopeful with French sweeties when he howls, and the Tamil coolie quenches his thirst out of the emptied milk tin.[89]

For Maeburn, white products in the East 'nourished' – both literally and figuratively – the childlike natives of savage frontiers whom he depicted as passive recipients of European help and European settler maternalism. However, Maeburn observed, nowhere on this scene was an Australian article to be found: 'The spirit of protection that wraps our country in the pall of commercial depression and death would never allow reciprocity with those favoured regions, and under no other conditions could a trade be possible.'[90] While Maeburn's fantasy of South Asian indigenous cultures suffused with Western goods was perhaps exaggerated, his frustration at Australia's economic disconnection from Asia echoed arguments that would be raised with the same irritation thirty years later during a second economic depression.

In 1933 Australian journalist J. H. C. Sleeman published the book *White China*, which, as I have argued elsewhere, was written in collaboration with Sydney's Chinese community.[91] In it he argued:

> If we are to trade with the East on equal terms, then we must have a greater measure of reciprocity between the nations. Bone fide merchants and their wives must be admitted to the Commonwealth on the same basis as our merchants and their wives were admitted to China . . . If we get preferential treatment for our goods in the East, then the products of the East must get similar preferences.[92]

Pointing to tensions within Australian trade policy in Asia, he elaborated:

> I cannot understand any man of any nation saying: 'Buy what we have to sell and keep out.' If the Japanese and Chinese are, in our opinion, below us, inferior things, then let us announce the fact, but do not let us demean

ourselves with soliciting trade from the people we banish from our shores and excommunicate from our counsels. For God's sake, let us be decent in our prejudices.[93]

He also called for what he termed 'other adjustments':

An old Chinese about to return to his native land, or about to die, must be given the right to maintain a successor. If a Chinese trader needs the assistance of a relative to help him in his business we must agree to the entry of such a person. If we exterminate the Chinese colony in Australia we eradicate all hope of an extension of trade with their Rip Van Winkle nation of the East, which, awaking from the carelessness of centuries, is demanding more equitable treatment as an unconditional necessity for international trade . . . In China, Australian products are condemned on account of unattractive labels . . . Australian exporters ignore suggestions regarding size and shape of tins and style of labels made by merchants in the East.[94]

Sleeman also drew on imperial tensions between Britain and Australia to get his point across. Expansion of Australian trade in China, he argued, was impossible until Australia had its currency on sale in the Orient. Until Australia could trade with China on an Australian pound basis, Australia would be 'kept out of the Big Game' by the operations of sterling and the juggling of other currencies.

The issue is, in the main, a political one, the assumed inferiority of the Australian to the Englishman, the inferiority of 'colonial' or 'dominion' institutions to those of the British Kingdom, is what is responsible.[95]

The very first essential to us successfully trading in the East is to play the game. Then we have to jettison a little of our overweening racial vanity. If we don't, well, then we will deserve all that is coming to us.[96]

By the 1930s, Australians returning to Australia from Asian trading posts were voicing similar critiques. Australia is the 'weakest link that binds Empire together', wrote Eldred Pottinger in 1928, 'and must get a better understanding of the Asian people . . . in Asia there is a growing feeling of "the East for the East" and a reluctance to regard the white man as necessarily superior in civilisation, learning, or religion'.[97] Writing in Australian newspapers, salesmen returning from China told of their problems setting up in trade. Australians 'seem to think that anything was good enough for the East', wrote Geoff Heath after returning from Hong Kong.[98] Major G. Adock was of the view that: 'We have tried to market our goods in the East without the most elementary investigation.'[99] Rex Phillips found his import and export business foundered when Australian customs officers slit his Chinese-made horse saddles to look for opium, 'When one hears about such acts as that being done, one begins to wonder if Australia isn't a good country to be out of.'[100] Thus, between the 1890s and the 1930s, a shift in power relations took place in Australian commercial encounters in Asia, with some Australian salespeople acknowledging the agency of Asian consumers who boycotted Australian products for cultural and anticolonial reasons.

Australian assumptions about Chinese inferiority were variously reproduced and undermined in the lives of Australian salesmen in interwar Shanghai. Chinese attitudes to Australian goods and Australians, as revealed in Chinese-language representations of Australians and Australian history, and British SMP attitudes to Australians, evident in existing special branch biographies and surveillance files, allow us to view this process at the level of commercial encounters played out in semi-colonial China. The existence of these transcolonial archives, in both Australia and China, raises questions about the causal connection between working-class aspirations for social mobility and job security during the Great Depression and Chinese awareness of and resentment towards the exclusionary and discriminatory practices of white settler societies. These archives also demonstrate the ways in which commercial encounters between Australian salespeople and local Chinese in Shanghai were open to resistance. It has been possible, however, to convey some of the response in China to their presence. What has been achieved here is an exploration of the ways in which salespeople exemplified overlaps between Australian and Asian commercial and colonial spaces in the 1920s and 1930s. Migratory histories of Australia typically assume white desires to 'protect' Australia's borders and Asian desires to cross these borders from Asia into Australia. This chapter has demonstrated the need to question scholarly investments in 'Destination Australia' through the examination of a problem population of white Australians in interwar Shanghai.

Despite a wealth of scholarship on Australian travel to China, little, if any, research has examined the transference of white Australians as *workers* into China. The journeys of Australian economic migrants during the Great Depression provide useful archival trails for historians in this regard. Precisely because commercial encounters operated under a fiction of equal exchange, they made European racism in these sites more visible. It was through these encounters that the reality of race-based inequality took its starkest form. White Australian 'convicts' were privileged as traders in Shanghai, while local Chinese, no matter what their class or social standing, were not. 'Whiteness' in these circumstances looked hollow and appeared to be based on little more than a fiction of inherited civility. Chinese resentment towards white colonial privilege was also manifest in Chinese responses to Australian products as Chinese consumers exercised their agency by boycotting Australian merchandise. In turn, Australian public debate over trade in the East was influenced by this rejection of Australian goods in China. By using Chinese-language sources to examine Chinese attitudes towards Australians in interwar Shanghai, we can begin to acknowledge the constitutive role of non-Western agency and knowledge in shaping domestic settler histories.

Notes

1   Speaker: Mr E. V. Elliot, Federal Secretary, Australian Seamen's Union, 4 September 1946, Friends of China Session, 'China Seamen's Union', Noel Butlin Archives, E183/21/38.

2   'Reports Made 1943–1945 during Japanese Occupation: Allan Willoughby Raymond Activities'. N.d. Shanghai Municipal Police Files, 1894–1945. US National Archives, Archives Unbound, Web, 1 March 2012. http://go.galegroup. com.rp.nla.gov.au/gdsc/i.do?&id=GALE%7CSC5100305550&v=2.1&u=nla &it=r&p=GDSC&sw=w&viewtype=fullcitation (accessed 2 March 2012).

3   Ibid.

4   Ibid.

5   'Files on Noulens Associates: Police Reports, Character Sketches and Newspaper'. N.d. Shanghai Municipal Police Files, 1894–1945. US National Archives, Archives Unbound, Web, 1 March 2012. http://go.galegroup.com.rp.nla.gov. au/gdsc/i.do?&id=GALE%7CSC5100304583&v=2.1&u=nla&it=r&p=GDSC &sw=w&viewtype=fullcitation (accessed 2 March 2012). See also: 'Reports of Special Branch Made Between 1929–1949: List of Licensed and Unlicensed Private Hotels Located South of Soochow Creek' [4 Folders]. N.d. Shanghai Municipal Police Files, 1894–1945, US National Archives, Archives Unbound, Web, 1 March 2012. http://go.galegroup.com.rp.nla.gov.au/gdsc/i.do?&id= GALE%7CSC5100168499&v=2.1&u=nla&it=r&p=GDSC&sw=w&viewtype= fullcitation (accessed 2 March 2012).

6   Ibid., 20.

7   Ibid., 19.

8   Isabella Jackson, 'The Raj on Nanjing Road: Sikh Policeman in Treaty-Port Shanghai', *Modern Asian Studies* 46 (2012): 11.

9   Lachlan Strahan, 'Treaty Ports and Missions', in Strahan, *Australia's China: Changing Perceptions from the 1930s to the 1990s* (Hong Kong: Cambridge University Press, 1996), 91–121.

10   Robert Bickers, 'Shanghailanders: The Formation and Identity of the British Settler Community in Shanghai', *Past and Present* 159 (May 1998): 193.

11   Antonia Finnane, *Far from Where? Jewish Journeys from Shanghai to Australia* (Carlton: University of Melbourne Press, 1999), 116.

12   Christian Henriot, 'Invisible Deaths, Silent Deaths: Bodies without Masters in Republican Shanghai', *Journal of Social History* (Winter 2009): 411.

13   Ibid., 117.

14   Papers of Rex, Clarence and Madge Phillips, 1924–1946, Manuscripts Collection, National Library of Australia (NLA), MS 9942.

15   'Files on Noulens Associates: Police Reports, Character Sketches and Newspaper . . .'.

16   Karl Gerth, *China Made: Consumer Culture and the Creation of the Nation* (Cambridge, MA: Harvard University Press, 2003), 126.

17   Li Jianhong, 'Beitong de Huigu (A Retrospective on Sorrow)', in Cao Muguan, *Lijie Guohuo zhanlanhui zhi jiguo* (The Ins-and-Outs of Successive National Products Exhibitions', Shanghai Municipal Archives (SMA) D2-0-2830-31; 'Humiliation Day', *North China Standard*, 5 October 1925; 'Angry Mob of Students Parade Streets of Peiking. Anti-foreign Demonstration', *Peking Leader*, 5 October 1925.

18   Karl Gerth, *China Made*, 127.

19   'Trade and Finance, Australia's Awful Name', *Western Mail*, 30 November 1922, 17.

20   J. H. C. Sleeman, *White China: An Austral-Asian Sensation* (Sydney: self-published, 1933), 285. See also: Sophie Loy-Wilson, 'Peanuts and Publicists:

"Letting Australian Friends Know the Chinese Side of the Story" in Interwar Sydney', *History Australia* 6.1 (2009): 1–20.

21 Sleeman, *White China*, 285. See also: A. C. V Melbourne, *Report on Australian Intercourse with Japan and China* (Brisbane: Frederick Phillips, 1932).

22 Sleeman, *White China*, 284.

23 'Advertising, Subsidies to Industries for Advertising', NAA A2489/1/1920/3344.

24 Greg Dening, 'Deep Times, Deep Spaces: Civilizing the Sea', in Bernhard Klein and Gesa Mackenthun (eds.) *Sea Changes: Historicizing the Ocean* (New York: Routledge, 2004), 13; R. H. Maeburn, 'Trade with the East: To the Editor', *Launceston Examiner*, 13 November 1894, 7.

25 Marilyn Lake and Henry Reynolds, *Drawing the Global Colour Line: White Men's Countries and the Question of Racial Equality* (Melbourne: Melbourne University Press, 2008), 15–49.

26 'Reports Made 1943–1945 during Japanese Occupation: Allan Willoughby Raymond Activities'.

27 Finnane, *Far from Where?*, 82.

28 'Reports Made 1943–1945 during Japanese Occupation: Allan Willoughby Raymond Activities'.

29 Ibid.

30 Ibid.

31 Ibid.

32 'Sidney Frank Hearne (British), Applicant for Enlistment in 1st Battalion, The Seaforth Highlanders'. N.d. Shanghai Municipal Police Files, 1894–1945, US National Archives, Archives Unbound, Web, 1 March 2012. http://go.galegroup.com.rp.nla.gov.au/gdsc/i.do?&id=GALE%7CSC5100436800&v=2.1&u=nla&it=r&p=GDSC&sw=w&viewtype=fullcitation (accessed 2 March 2012); 'Boyle, R. H. (Nick) and H. (Harry) Kerrey. Reports Made 1943–1945 during Japanese Occupation: R. H. (Nick) Boyle And H. (Harry) Kerrey'. N.d. Shanghai Municipal Police Files, 1894–1945, US National Archives, Archives Unbound, Web, 1 March 2012. http://go.galegroup.com.rp.nla.gov.au/gdsc/i.do?&id=GALE%7CSC5100283512&v=2.1&u=nla&it=r&p=GDSC&sw=w&viewtype=fullcitation (accessed 2 March 2012).

33 'Commercial Intelligence, China', NAA A11804/1/1927/47.

34 Finnane, *Far from Where?*, 86.

35 'Boyle, R. H. (Nick) and H. (Harry) Kerrey. Reports Made 1943–1945 during Japanese Occupation'.

36 Ibid.

37 Ibid.

38 Finnane, *Far from Where?*, 107.

39 'Ivers, Jack Edward. Files on Noulens Associates: Jack Edward Ivers'. N.d. Shanghai Municipal Police Files, 1894–1945. US National Archives. Archives Unbound. Web. 1 March 2012. http://go.galegroup.com.rp.nla.gov.au/gdsc/i.do?&id=GALE%7CSC5100266094&v=2.1&u=nla&it=r&p=GDSC&sw=w&viewtype=fullcitation (accessed 2 March 2012).

40 Ibid.

41 Ibid.

42 Ibid.

43 Ibid.

44 Tony Ballantyne and Antoinette Burton, 'Introduction', in Ballantyne and Burton (eds.) *Bodies in Contact: Rethinking Colonial Encounters in World History* (Durham, NC: Duke University Press, 2005), 12.

45 'Sidney Frank Hearne (British), Applicant for Enlistment in 1st Battalion, The Seaforth Highlanders'.

46 Ibid.
47 Ibid.
48 Ibid.
49 Henry Champly, *The Road to Shanghai: White Slave Traffic in Asia*, translated from the French by Warre B. Wells (London: John Long, 1932), 12.
50 Ibid., 131.
51 'Commercial Intelligence, China'.
52 'China – Foreign Concessions', NAA A981/4 CHIN 61; Tiensin British Committee of Information, Memorandum No. 1 Foreign Settlements and Concessions in China, NAA A981/4 CHIN 19.
53 Ibid.
54 *Report of the Hon Mr. Justice Feetham to the Shanghai Municipal Council*, vol. 1 (Shanghai, 1931), 5, NLA, MS 4441; William C. Johnstone, 'The Feetham Report: A New Plan for Shanghai', *American Political Science Review* 25.4 (November 1931): 1047.
55 'China – Foreign Concessions'; Tiensin British Committee of Information, Memorandum No. 1.
56 Tiensin British Committee of Information, Memorandum No. 1.
57 Ibid.
58 Li Jianhong, 'Beitong de Huigu (A Retrospective on Sorrow)'. See also: Li Chien-Min, 五卅惨案後的反英運動 (Anti-British Movement after the May Thirtieth Movement 1925–1926) (Taipei, Republic of China: Institute of Modern History Academica Sinica, 1986).
59 'Changing Attitudes of the Chinese towards Foreigners in China' (Ji'nan, 28 March 1923), American Consulate of Shanghai (ACS) File 893.4974:4.
60 'Changing Attitudes of the Chinese towards Foreigners in China' (Chifou, 7 April 1923), ACS File 893.4972.
61 ACS File 893.4973 (Hankou, 2 April 1923), 2–3.
62 Ibid.
63 Copy from the *People's Tribune* (February 1936), newspaper cuttings in the Beatrice Thompson papers, NAA Box 29 1948/732 SP 104/1.
64 Champly, *Road to Shanghai*, 120.
65 Emphasis in original. Papers of Rex, Clarence and Madge Phillips.
66 Ibid.
67 '中英談判' (Chinese–British Negotiations), *Criticism Journal* (時評), SMA D2-0-973; 'Australia' (奧州), *Eastern Magazine* (*Dongfang Zhouzhi*, 東方周知) 31.2 (1935): 47, SMA D2-0-1471-67.
68 Ibid., 47.
69 Ibid.
70 '中英談判' (Chinese–British Negotiations); 'Australia' (奧州), *Eastern Magazine*, 47. For a discussion of *guanzhan* discourse in Republican-era China see: Yamin Xu, 'Policing Civility on the Streets: Encounters with Litterbugs, "Nightsoil Lords" and Street Corner Urinators in Republican Beijing', *Twentieth Century China* 30.2 (April 2005): 28–71.
71 Diane Kirkby, '"Honorary Chinese?" Women Citizens, Whiteness and Labour Legislation in the Early Australian Commonwealth', *Social Identities* 13.6 (2007): 804.
72 'Australia' (澳州), *Global Half-Annual Journal* (*Huan Qiu Xun Kan*, 還球旬刊), 37 (1931): 37, SMA D2-0-2830-37.
73 Ibid., 37.
74 Ibid., 39.
75 Ibid., 40.
76 'What I Found in Australia Because of the Game', SMA D2-0-1471-67, 56.

77 Ibid., 57.
78 T. K. Tseng (Tseng Tsung-chien) to George Morrison, Melbourne, Victoria, Australia, 12 October 1914; see: *The Correspondence of G. E. Morrison* (Cambridge and New York: Cambridge University Press, 1976–1978), 348–349.
79 'Australian Trade with China, the East and the Pacific Islands General', NAA CP703/5/23/A5131; letter from V. J. Palstra, 18 June 1931, Far Eastern Representative Salesman, Shanghai, to Mr Moore, Premier of Queensland Commerce – China, NAA A461/9/1323/1/5.
80 Letter from V. J. Palstra, 18 June 1931.
81 Ibid.
82 Ibid.
83 Ibid.
84 Ibid.
85 Ibid.; Memorandum, Department of Markets, E. J. Mulvany, Secretary, 20 November 1931, 'Australian Trade with China, the East and the Pacific Islands General', NAA CP703/5/23/A5131.
86 Letter from V. J. Palstra, 18 June 1931.
87 House of Representatives, 31 August 1931, 'Australian Trade with China Commerce – China', NAA A461/9/1323/1/5; 'Australian Trade with China, the East and the Pacific Islands General'; Publicity, NEI Australian News for China, NAA A457/1/G532/4.
88 Champly, *Road to Shanghai*, 117.
89 R. H. Maeburn, 'Trade with the East: To the Editor', *Launceston Examiner*, 13 November 1894, 7.
90 Ibid.
91 Sleeman, *White China*. See also: Loy-Wilson, 'Peanuts and Publicists', 1–20.
92 Sleeman, *White China*, 303.
93 Ibid., 290.
94 Ibid., 303.
95 Ibid., 279.
96 Ibid., 303.
97 'Australia and Asia, Asiatic Problems Affecting Australia', *The Register*, 18 August 1928, 4. See also: H. Francessen, 'East for Trade: A Plea for a Wider Vision', *Rydge's Business Journal* (1 September 1932): 527–532.
98 'A Footing in the East: Australian Traders Given Advice', *Barrier Miner*, 6 April 1933, 1.
99 Major G. Adock, 'What Does the East Offer the Business Man?', *Rydge's Business Journal* (August 1933): 686.
100 Papers of Rex, Clarence and Madge Phillips.

Part III
'Liberating' China, 'Saving' Australia

5 Socialists, Missionaries and Internationalists

When we change from day to night shift, we have to work sixteen hours . . . Ah!
When will we be treated as the European workers? We may be called the factory
animals of the world of darkness.[1]

Petition from workers at the Lungwa cement factory,
Twelfth Year of the Chinese Republic (1923)

Testimony from Shanghai's Lungwa factory, and from workers in China and India
made its way into the trade literature of Australian unions in the 1920s. Sent by
missionary and socialist groups across Asia into trade hall offices, quoted in the
Australian Federal parliament, read aloud at meetings, and reprinted in pamphlets
and trade newspapers, voices from colonial factories ran down the rungs of labour
media, incorporating the localised and often stifled demands of Australian
unionists into a worldwide campaign for the 'dignity of labour' and the 'liberation
of Asia'. Contained in the scrapbooks of union leaders are the letters that followed
these petitions (from Li Hung Ling in Shanghai and Gopal Singh in Delhi), which
carefully pressed home points of shared labour principles (a basic wage, a pension
scheme), while avoiding racial divides along the empire colour line.[2] Without
'union solidarity' against the forces of capital, all would become 'factory animals
of the world of darkness'.

The central role played by trade unionism in the politics of the interwar period
has been well established. This chapter revisits the activities of Australian trade
unions in the twentieth century and looks at the unexpected ways in which
trade union media chose to represent unionism to the Australian public during
these years. Analysing interwar unionism at this register reveals surprising
connections between metropolitan Australian trade unions and Shanghai-based
anticolonial protest movements.

Having battled for and won improved conditions for workers in the years before
1916, unions in Australia, and worldwide, watched these achievements erode by
the end of the First World War.[3] In response, workplace leaders organised
increasingly desperate and violent strike action: bread riots in Melbourne in 1919,
coal strikes in Queensland and police strikes in Victoria in 1923, a seamen's strike
across imperial ports (from South Africa to Perth to Hong Kong) in 1925, and

the general strike in England in 1926.[4] Australian strike activity peaked in 1917 with 5 million workdays lost, nearly ten times the days lost to industrial action in 1913. While strikes tapered off in 1918, they surged again in 1919 and 1920. This level of industrial action was not experienced again in Australia until the mid-1940s.[5]

Running parallel to these industrial conflicts was another form of popular agitation, as colonised peoples protested against British rule across Asia. In 1919 British troops killed 400 Indian protesters at Amritsar, and in 1925 Shanghai Municipal Police (SMP) officers shot into a crowd of Chinese unionists in Shanghai.[6] One unexpected result of the Shanghai shootings was the sudden reaction by some Australian factory workers, who quickly likened their own struggle against 'imperial capitalism' to the protests in Shanghai and other parts of Asia. Chinese workers had similar feelings, telling British officials: '*Australia is like China*, a nation oppressed by the British race.'[7] Australian unions tapped into the resulting global outrage over the Shanghai incident, fashioning local support for labour rights in sympathy with Shanghai. The street deaths in China were perceived as echoing government brutality towards strikers in Australia, giving unions an Asian regional mythology through which to articulate the plight of workers. They did so against the shifting sands of Pacific relations, as British moral legitimacy weakened at its eastern reach, and the bonds of imperial trade and preferential tariffs for British goods confronted a new economic order.[8] Australia needed new markets and new investors as Britain withdrew but, to move forward, outdated attitudes had to be reappraised; Asian 'coolies' were becoming Asian 'customers'.[9] At the same time, international organisations such as the Young Women's Christian Association (YWCA) and the International Labour Organisation (ILO) promoted the cause of Chinese labour rights, leading to global debates over the need to regulate labour in Chinese factories and address inequalities between 'Eastern' and 'Western' working conditions in the plastic days of China's industrial development.

While interwar strike action and Pan-Asian self-determination movements have both been the subject of much scholarly scrutiny, the alignment between the two – the affiliations and shared promotional activities linking anticolonial resistance with unionism – has lain between the boundaries of distinct academic fields, and this is especially true for Australian history.[10] Although Heather Goodall and Julia Martinez have questioned orthodox histories of Australian union isolationism and xenophobia by tracing cross-racial mateship in the Chinese-dominated Darwin Seamen's Union and the Sydney Indian Seamen's Union, the wider impact of Asian nationalism on domestic Australian politics remains largely unresearched.[11] Marilyn Lake and Henry Reynold's work in *Drawing the Global Colour Line* is an exception and has spurred historical examinations of the 'transnational solidarities' linking Australia to Asia.[12] As Gregor Benton has written in his analyses of Chinese migrant internationalism, scholars are now 'having a fresh look at unions and "non-white" labour and finding that there is more to this story than labour racism'.[13] In this chapter I do not argue that affiliation between Australian and Chinese factory workers proves that Australian unions supported decolonisation in the 1920s. Rather, by tracing connections between Sydney and Shanghai, in what Wang Gungwu has called 'the era of labour and socio-revolutionary internationalism', I engage with two main questions.[14] First, how did unions in Australia come to make a case for workers' rights, which – by spotlighting the treatment of workers in treaty port China – carried a critique of 'Britishness'? And second, what changes to distinctions of class and race made this argument possible in an Australian community fiercely proud of empire, which vilified 'nigger labour' and refused union membership to the 'coloured races'? Chapter 2 demonstrated that promotional culture is a fruitful way into the relationship between politics and gender in the 1920s and 1930s. So I turn my attention to the connection between class and race and suggest that anticolonial protest movements taking place in the wider Asian region informed domestic Australian conceptions of class-based inequality. In the process, the lives of factory workers in Sydney and Shanghai were temporarily and unexpectedly entwined.

***

In August 1925 an Australian in China, 'in the course of an afternoon's ramble', inadvertently walked into the middle of a Hong Kong strike. The Chinese strikers, assuming the man was English and therefore an 'imperial capitalist', detained him under the watch of Punjabi guards.[15] On mentioning that he was Australian, the man was immediately released, the Chinese declaring: '*Australia is like China, a nation oppressed by the British race*; we have no quarrels with Australians, but only with the British.'[16] The Australian made his way out from behind the strikers' fortifications and cabled the Department of External Affairs in Canberra with the tale. Australian officials quickly circulated transcripts of his call, underlining the words 'Australia is like China' with tense, red pencil strokes.[17] Here was a small story articulating larger racial and spatial tensions. British-owned and run Hong Kong exemplified the annexing of Chinese sovereign territory by European powers – what was known in China as the 'carving of the melon' (*gua fen*).[18] Like other treaty port cities along China's coastline (Guangzhou, Amoy, Shanghai, Chefoo), Hong Kong was a boom town for European manufacturing. Chinese workers filled factories that multiplied in a concession environment favourable to capitalist enterprise, offering plentiful labour, little regulation, low wages and preferential tariffs for British goods. In the mid-1920s strike action was causing regular stoppages, and anti-British feeling was intensifying.[19] By declaring affinity with Australia, Hong Kong's strikers articulated an unexpected strand of Chinese anticolonial logic: Britain should not only leave China, they argued; Britain should also leave Asia, *all* of Asia, even 'White Australia'. Gregor Benton has shown how international alliances across Australasian racial divides sprang from the spontaneous perception by Chinese and other non-Chinese migrants of shared problems in everyday life and work.[20] Drawing on Australia's and China's common experience of modern imperialism, unionists in Hong Kong ignored distinctions between different slabs of imperial real estate – 'Dominion', 'treaty port', 'colony', 'concession' – forming a new basis for building commonality across Asia, and across the cultural and hierarchical boundaries of empire.

Between 1925 and 1929 strike violence and government crackdowns in Australia appeared to echo a series of dramatic events taking place in China and, particularly, in Shanghai, which allowed Australian union leaders to use the city as a stage on which to dramatise and justify their methods in Australia. On Saturday 30 May 1925 Kenneth John McEuen, SMP commissioner, received word that a demonstration had been called by student unionists to protest against the killing of a Chinese worker, named Gu Zhenghong, by a textile factory guard.[21] A crowd of 'several hundred, increasing all the time', swelled onto Shanghai's main shopping thoroughfare, Nanjing Road, stopped outside the front of Wing On Department Store in order to hear a speaker, and then headed for the Louza police station.[22] The crowd appeared to come to a standstill outside the Town Hall. Missionary Harry Westnidge found himself swallowed up in a crush of bodies: 'They were not going back and not going forward; then there was a shower of pamphlets and papers of all description coming southwards along Chekiang Road. I could see the flags and leaflets being thrown up in the air. This appeared to put new heart in the surge.'[23] The crowd continued on and surrounded the station. At this point SMP officers standing inside claimed to hear 'Kill the foreigners' shouted in both English and Chinese.[24] They reacted and shot into the crowd, killing several and leaving more wounded. Blood-spattered white shirts taken from the bodies of the dead were photographed and slid into the pages of papers across the globe, aided by the increasing reach of media agencies such as Reuters and Hassan.[25] Further protests broke out across China, and these repeated street actions attracted the title 'May 30th Movement'. An inquiry and public trial ensued, with transcripts being published for popular consumption.[26]

For most of 1925 China would be the 'cynosure' of the world, as the 'Shanghai incident' ('Britain's biggest catastrophe in Asia since Amritsar') became a 'test for Empire' and international opinion rallied to support Chinese demands for freedom and self-determination.[27] Public sympathy had been turning against the British presence in China for some time, with the media increasingly depicting the colonial Orient as immoral, lambasting treaty port 'Shanghailanders as parasitic and cruel exploiters of Chinese labor and violent defenders of their privilege'.[28] Since 1922 the YWCA – with Rockefeller Foundation money – had been running a successful 'public opinion' campaign against child slavery in British-owned factories in China and India.[29] In Australia, the 'rising tide of color' would collide with 'the rising tide of labor', as Asian calls for an end to empire were made local, challenging the way unionists conceptualised political action and also what it meant to identify as British and Australian.[30]

In Sydney, Labor Party members lectured on the 'Shanghai trouble', likening the British presence in China to territorial robbery. At one public meeting, a Labor speaker asked the crowd: 'How would you like it if someone came and took Sydney off us?'[31] Eyewitness accounts of May 30th, written by Australian missionaries in Shanghai, were passed out by the YWCA: 'Some of the students were weeping and blood was streaming from their heads and faces . . . In running

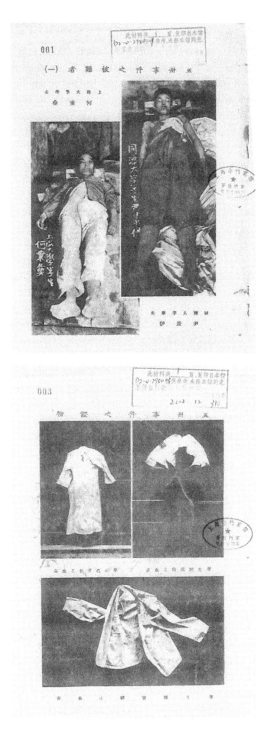

Figure 5.1 The bodies and the clothes of the 'May 30th Martyrs'.

Source: Shanghai Municipal Archives (SMA) D2-02-14-154.

pools of blood there were some 10 or 12 boys and men, dead and dying.' Such profound interest was made possible by an already existing belief that British factory managers mistreated Chinese workers. This was bolstered by residual nineteenth-century popular narratives, which figured colonial capitalists as akin to slave owners, practising barbarous acts away from the reforming gaze of metropolitan regulators. Rumours about Indian and Chinese workers abounded:

> Indian workers were 'blown from cannons for British sport' and 'Chinese workers averaged one meal a day'; '32 million Indian natives had died from starvation' and 'British factory owners mixed opium into the food of their workers'. This was 'so that his loyalty to Britain is quite passingly submissive and he seldom smiles'.[32]

There was also the fear that Shanghai illustrated life without unions, prophesying a potential future for Australian workers if union membership continued to erode, and the Bruce government was successful in its efforts to dismantle wage arbitration.

Beginning in the early 1920s, church and union groups that linked Australia to the Far East had arranged for descriptions of factory life in Shanghai and other parts of Asia to be distributed in Australia. Labour newspapers sympathetic to international socialism published the resulting reports. In these articles, a shared 'film of empire' linked Asian and white factory workers together against morally bankrupt British bosses. A sense of similarity, of Dominion lives lived out in parallel but in very different worlds, could evade thorny questions of race, making it possible for trade union papers to run this news about Indian, Filipino and Chinese factory workers without alienating their Australian readers, or becoming embroiled in a debate over 'coloured labour'. As early as 1921 the *Northern Standard* (the newly established newspaper of the North Australian Industrial Union) wrote of the 'awakening' of Chinese, Indian, Japanese and Filipino workers in a 'struggle to free themselves from the shackles of bondage'.[33]

In February 1925 *One Big Union* ran an article entitled 'Two Unionists Beheaded in Public: British Commander Orders the Execution of Two Innocent Men'.[34] The article told the story of the night of 19 June 1924, when the drowned body of Edwin C. Hawley was pulled out of Shanghai Harbour. Hawley's corpse was then dragged onto a British gunboat that was making its way, as usual, up and down the wharfside, throwing a conspicuous shadow across Shanghai's docklands. Assuming Hawley had been 'beaten and thrown into the water by Chinese junk-men', the ship's commander ordered Chinese authorities to behead two officials from the Shanghai Junkman's Union on the wharves. Without 'any investigation' and 'after futile protests from a Chinese magistrate', two union leaders were taken to a beach off the docklands and promptly executed, 'a perfect sample of the kind of British justice obtained in China at this time'.[35] At the side of this article, *One Big Union* published an illustration that showed 'money' in suit and tails, whip in hand, forcing men to jump off the wharves, while the allegorical Starvation watched on and the Great Wall of China rose on the horizon. These reports were not unusual. Grisly tales of union beheadings sat alongside descriptions of rough British treatment of Chinese civilians. In April 1925 the *Seamen's Journal* reported that a Mr Gumley, of the British firm Butterfield & Squires, had pushed a Chinese man 'somewhat rudely' off his seat in a tugboat in Guangzhou and had to apologise publicly under threat of a strike by all Butterfield & Squires' workers.[36]

A string of missionary works and lecture tours that was launched in Australia in the early 1920s reiterated the argument that China's struggle against Britain was a humanitarian struggle against capitalism. Adelaide Anderson and Agatha Harrison of the YWCA toured Australia in 1923 and 1928, calling for 'the support of the Australian people in a campaign to save China from some of the horrors [British] people went through during the Industrial Revolution'.[37] Anderson described a

> situation [in China] that beggared description . . . factories were developing a 1921 industrial organization with 1800 conditions for men, women and children . . . the conditions that accompanied the growth of English industrial history are known to you all, so you can picture China [in all its] hideous spectacle.[38]

The women's speeches were 'aimed at rousing [*sic*] hearers' to 'a sense of responsibility' as 'we Westerners have so much to answer for. We brought the industrial system [to China].'[39]

The early twentieth century was the height of the internationalising period of the Young Men's Christian Association (YMCA) and the YWCA – called the Y movement for short – which saw close ties form between mission work and labour rights advocacy.[40] At an industrial conference in 1923, Australian unions had passed a resolution to cooperate with the Y: 'To organize a publicity campaign through the city and country press and devise the ways and means by which this can be carried out.'[41] George Waite, head of the Seamen's Union, urged delegates 'to discuss the practicality of coordinating forces [with the Y] and to formulate, or take the necessary steps to formulate, a general message for propaganda purposes'.[42] The Y movement had begun as an evangelical mission to the urban working classes in London in 1844, with branches opening in New York in the 1850s, Melbourne in the 1880s and Shanghai in 1912.[43] By 1925 the Y operated over fifty city and country outlets in Australia.[44] Between 1922 and 1923 the Shanghai Y was in talks with the Rockefeller Foundation, eventually receiving substantial funding to spend on 'creating public opinion' and 'sympathy' for the exploitation of labour in China, and to agitate for the 'reform of International Labor legislation'. According to one Y pamphlet: 'At this moment China is the cynosure of all eyes – and the world is waiting on the industrial situation there. A still more significant fact is that Labor in other countries is watching with a growing concern for the people involved.' The Shanghai Y were given $4,487 by the Rockefeller Foundation, $800 of which they spent on publicity and literature; much of this made its way to Australian Y outlets, and also to union offices.[45]

In early 1925 Sydney welfare officer and factory inspector Eleanor Hinder was made a secretary at the Y's Shanghai office. Known for her work as a welfare officer in department store factories, Hinder was closely involved in Sydney's labour world and had written one of the first union pamphlets for female department store workers.[46] In Shanghai she met Viola Smith, who had been a member of the editorial staff of the ILO at its inaugural conference in Washington and had also held a position in the Child Labor Division of the US Department of Labor.[47] Their friendship would cement the connection between Y work on Shanghai and the ILO.[48] Once in China, and right in the mad grit and sprawl of Shanghai's Zhabei factory district, Hinder kept a grip on her Australian connections through correspondence with friends and family, and by sending home Y pamphlets and photographs documenting Chinese labour conditions. Along with other Australian-born missionaries, she had begun visiting factories in Shanghai in 1923.[49] Dominating a dusty flat area between the Yangtze River and Shanghai's red-light district, Zhabei was a cheek-to-cheek expanse of flat, mile-long manufacturing sheds and slum alleys.[50] As Hinder recorded:

> The dust was appalling. I noticed that the man who took us around (he has financial interest in the factory) went through the rooms with a handkerchief over his nose and mouth. The workers spend their LIVES in this atmosphere. The scene was unforgettable.[51]

Australia's Trade Commissioner in Shanghai shared her concerns: 'Conditions prevailing are horrifying. Little girls of the tenderest age arrive between 4am and 6am to begin their day shift. Women bring their babies and put them on the mill floor to sleep.' The cause was 'Western industrialism' which had 'gripped the country and is here to stay'.[52] Among these workers were large numbers of women and children, used mostly in steam filatures, cigarette factories, textile factories and hosiery mills. Eleanor Hinder was so repelled by the degrading physical torture of these women and children that she began a campaign to 'ameliorate their deplorable conditions':[53]

> The coming of modern industry to China has been described as a terrific invasion and this modern revolution in China is taking place so quietly that few people are aware that anything untoward is happening . . . these industries in foreign owned concession cities such as Shanghai do not come under the law of the homeland – England, America or France for instance – nor do they make any voluntary attempt to live up to such laws. I found more willingness on the part of Chinese employers to do the right thing than on the part of foreign employers.[54]

Factories became well-established illustrations of industrial capitalism in the interwar years. According to Roland Marchland, the 1920s and 1930s were the 'era of the factory photograph', when corporations 'strove to make showplaces of their factories' through the widespread circulation of industrial images.[55]

During these years, corporations more than doubled the number of commissions of factory photographs.[56] The Y in Shanghai adopted this technique for different ends in the 1920s, using industrial photography in their exposés of Zhabei. In November 1924 the Shanghai Y published *The Long Hard Day in China*, documenting 'factory life' in Zhabei.[57] Elizabeth Christman, of the National Women's Trade Union League of America, organised the distribution of *Long Hard Day* in Britain and America, while Hinder arranged supplies for Australia. Both women targeted labour and union leaders such as Herbert McDonnell, head of the British Labour Party, and Billy Hughes, former Labor prime minister of Australia (1915–1928): 'We are sending you copies of *The Life and Labor Bulletin* [as well as] *The Long Hard Day in China* picturing so vividly the working conditions . . . which are so challenging to our Western Civilization.'[58] Included in the literature were images of very young children:

> One is a small boy of ten who was brought in the other morning with his lips torn to ribbons and his jaw almost fractured because after a twelve hour night shift he had fallen against the machinery at four am and he has worked under these conditions since he was a baby of seven. The other is a seventeen-year-old girl who, during a shift of twelve and a half hours, wavered near the flying wheels and had her scalp torn from her head. These are the facts – they hardly sound real.[59]

In order to gain access to Zhabei, foreign YWCA women enlisted the help of Chinese members, who collected and translated the testimonials of workers. In Lungwa cement factory Li Hung Ling and Wu Chien Fu handed missionaries a petition, which was also included in Y booklets:

> We have no seats while we work . . . When we change from day to night shift, we have to work sixteen hours – four hours more than usual . . . Ah! When will we be treated as the European workers? We may be called the factory animals of the world of darkness.[60]

The *Long Hard Day in China* and other pamphlets elicited international condemnation of Britain's role in China and protest from Labour members in the British parliament and throughout the world. Hinder reported in the YWCA newsletter *Threads* that W. M. ('Billy') Hughes 'both cabled and wrote' from Australia to the British Parliament, as did other labour leaders from Britain, America, Japan, India, Czechoslovakia and France.[61] She mused that the Y was now leading a 'social revolution' in labour rights:

> International Action is remarkably new to all of us and the first casting of small threads across the spaces that divide us may seem as futile as the spider's light filament. But watch them by degrees strengthen into unbreakable bonds. A weaving has started that cannot easily be stopped . . . Slogans and posters and handbills, in terms people can understand, distributed and broadcast at such times, have led to common thinking and engendered a group mind.[62]

TAKEN FOR THE CHILD LABOR CAMPAIGN, JUST
AS SHE CAME OUT FROM A COTTON
MILL IN SHANGHAI

Figure 5.2 'Taken for the Child Labor Campaign, just as she came out from a
cotton mill in Shanghai'.

Source: Facing title page in 'Threads: The Story of the Industrial Work of the YWCA in
China'.

As Zhabei's infamy grew, attention moved from factory workers to factory owners, and to the activities of foreign firms based in China. Y publicity quoted British factory managers on the use of child labour: 'If we stop employing children our mills will have to close down'; 'Children's hands are peculiarly suited to this work.'[63]

The topic was debated in the British Parliament in 1924:

> We are not oblivious of the fact – we are well aware of it – that the war has done other things than smash up international relations. It has been the forcing ground for industrialism in countries that were previously agricultural. We know that that has to be faced, but I comment to this house this point of view – that to equalise labour conditions we will have to give more and more attention not merely to British trade but perhaps to British investors. I have in mind the situation that is growing up in China and I have been informed that many of those mills have been started up by British and American capital – and yet the conditions of those mills are worse than those at the beginning of our own factory system.[64]

The emotive linkage of childhood to paid work triggered anticapitalist critiques in Britain and Australia, providing trade unions with a new visual vocabulary ('these atrocities of international imperialism') in which to describe Australian 'factory lives'.[65]

Angela Woollacott has shown that, for Australian interwar travellers like Eleanor Hinder, class relationships mediated encounters with colonised people because 'anticolonial nationalism helped them to recognise the role of empire in the production of poverty and suffering'.[66] I would add to Woollacott's argument by suggesting that organisations like the YWCA extended this recognition of the link between poverty and empire to a domestic Australian audience. Attracting a broad spread of devotees, garnering respectable and wealthy patronage and opening outlets and youth halls at an exponential rate, the Y provided a much needed distribution network for Australian unionism and anticolonial protest movements. Flush with funds, real estate and connections, Y secretaries such as Eleanor Hinder, Adelaide Anderson and Agatha Harrison plugged Australasian trade unions into an immense international publicity machine with modern communication systems and growing appeal.[67]

China's first Factory Act, 1931

In Shanghai in 1931 the ILO, working with the YWCA, the International Federation of Women and the Chinese government, promulgated China's first Factory Act. The Factory Law was aimed at promoting the cooperation of capitalists and labourers in matters of mutual interest, and at elevating the position of labourers to enable them to 'compete in the labour market of the world'.[68] Its efficacy was immediately limited by the complex territorial organisation of treaty port space.

In 1931, three months after the promulgation of the Act, Eleanor Hinder took fellow internationalist Rewi Alley with her on a series of factory inspections of Chinese-owned factories in the International Settlement. She subsequently wrote a critical letter to Albert Thomas at the ILO, noting that 'most of them are very far from safe':

> One rubber show factory is especially dangerous. Gasoline is in use, in open cans, practically throughout, as a solvent of Rubber, the stairways are rough, wooden, as well as the upper floors. There are many workers on the rickety upper floors, and in case of a fire hardly any workers could escape. Alongside is a crowded cigarette factory equally or more dangerous structurally. I cannot rest while I think of these workers and only the continuous vigilance of the Brigade Officers can save any of them if fire once starts. Under the Chinese Factory Law ss. 41(4) & 44 what can be done in the International Settlement? In the Chinese Settlement there would be a practical solution. But in the International Settlement the Officers can under existing powers apparently only urge, not compel, the owners.[69]

Eleanor Hinder, Albert Thomas of the ILO and the Chinese government exchanged a series of letters, condemning evasions of the Factory Act, with the Shanghai Municipal Council general managers. The Shanghai Municipal Council replied to Thomas and stated in their defence:

> The authorities and the inspector in the course of enforcing the Factory Law and carrying out the inspection work should show sympathy to the factories in order that such inspection may not be so rigid as to render it contrary to the spirit of the law. The enforcement of the Factory Law is a matter of life and death to the industries of China. The political and economic conditions of the country will be greatly affected by it. If you could see to it that the Ministry of Industry is requested to give the matter serious consideration, and try to comply with the request of the Association.[70]

Thinking inequality through China

The problem of child slavery and poor working conditions in Chinese factories drew international attention in the interwar period, generating debate among internationalists over how best to regulate labour in a country fissured into foreign concessions by European colonialism. In Shanghai in 1931 the ILO, working with the YWCA, the International Federation of Women and the Chinese government, promulgated China's first Factory Act. Australian socialists, missionaries and internationalists were central to this process. The factory laws aimed at gaining the cooperation of capitalists and labourers in matters of mutual interest and elevating the position of labourers to enable them to 'compete in the labour market of the world'. By tracing the origins of this Factory Act through circles of Australians in treaty port Shanghai, we can follow the economic ideologies foundational to the Act through a number of different iterations: from national to international, global to local. Reading these economic theories through the broader history of factory inspection and anticolonial union activism in Australia and China reveals that this history shaped global debates over labour inequality and imperial capitalism in twentieth-century Australia and China.

Notes

1 Petition addressed to Dame Adelaide Anderson from workers at the Lungwa cement factory, 13 December, Twelfth Year of the Chinese Republic (1923), Eleanor Hinder papers 1897–1963, Mitchell Library (ML), MS 770, Box 20.
2 George Waite papers, ML MS 208; Eleanor Hinder papers. See also: Marilyn Lake and Henry Reynolds, *Drawing the Global Colour Line: White Men's Countries and the Question of Racial Equality* (Melbourne: Melbourne University Press, 2008).
3 Vere Gordon Childe, *How Labour Governs: A Study of Workers Representation in Australia* (Parkville: Melbourne University Press, 1964, first published 1923); Jim Hagan, *The History of the A.C.T.U.* (Melbourne: Longman Cheshire, 1981), in particular 'The Challenge to Laborism', 15–25; P. W. D. Mathews and G. W. Ford (eds.) *Australian Trade Unions: Their Development, Structure and Horizons* (Melbourne: Sun Books, 1968), 35; Margo Beasley, *Wharfies: A History of the Waterside Workers' Federation of Australia* (Sydney: Halstead Press, 1996), in particular '1917–1927: Strikes, Riots and Labour Bureaus', 45–103.
4 Some 6.3 million days were lost to strikes in Australia in 1919 alone. See: Beasley, *Wharfies*, 53; Brian Fitzpatrick and Rowan J. Cahill, *The Seamen's Union of Australia* (Sydney: Star Printery, 1981), 50–59.
5 John Pragnell Bradley, '"Selling Consent": From Authoritarianism to Welfarism at David Jones, 1838–1958', PhD Thesis, University of New South Wales, 2001, 56.
6 Jon Lawrence, 'Forging a Peaceable Kingdom: War, Violence and Fear of Brutalization in Post-First World War Britain', *Journal of Modern History* 75.3 (September 2003): 557–589. See also: Richard W. Rigby, *The May 30th Movement: Events and Themes* (Canberra: Australian National University Press, 1980).
7 My emphasis. To the Director of the Pacific Branch, Prime Minister's Department, Melbourne, from Major General Commanding H.R.M. Troops in China, 'China Command Intelligence Diary for June 1925', Secret JG 533/5, NAA A10915/1/1. See also: 'Publications – Shanghai Publicity Bureau "News Bulletins"', NAA A981/PUB78; 'China – Anti-foreign Movement', NAA A981/4 CHIN 48; 'External Affairs Department – China, Who's Who', NAA A981/4 CHIN 152 PART 1; 'China – Foreign Concessions', NAA A981/4 CHIN 61.
8 A. G. Hopkins, 'Rethinking Decolonization', *Past and Present* 200.1 (2008): 211–247; Robert Bickers, *Britain in China: Community, Culture and Colonialism* (Manchester: Manchester University Press, 1999), 35–36; Nicholas Clifford, *Spoilt Children of Empire: Westerners in Shanghai and the Chinese Revolution of the 1920s* (Hanover, NH: Middlebury College Press, 1991). On the Imperial tariff system see: Angela Redish, 'British Financial Imperialism after the First World War', in Raymond E. Dumett (ed.) *Gentlemanly Capitalism and British Imperialism* (London: Longman, 1999), 127–140.
9 Julia Martinez, 'Internationalism between Australian and Asian Seamen', in Raymond Markey (ed.) *Labour and Community: Historical Essays* (Wollongong: University of Wollongong Press, 2001), 295–313. See also: Julia Martinez, 'Coolies to Comrades: Internationalism between Australian and Asian Seamen', in Ray Markey (ed.) *Labour and Community: Historical Essays* (Wollongong: University of Wollongong Press, 2001), 295–312.

10 This is a simplification of a complex academic debate. Transnational and comparative works are currently redressing this division. See: Lake and Reynolds, *Drawing the Global Colour Line*, especially chapter 6 'White Australia Points the Way', 137–166; Devleena Ghosh, Heather Goodall and S. J. Donald, *Water, Borders and Sovereignty in Asia and Oceania* (London: Routledge, 2008); Devleena Ghosh, *Colonialism and Modernity: History and Themes* (Sydney: University of NSW Press, 2007); Nick Dyrenfurth and Marion Quartly, '"All the World Over": The Transnational Labours of Early Australian Radical Cartoonists, 1886–1918', in M. Quartly and R. Scully (eds.) *Drawing the Line* (Melbourne: Monash University ePress, 2009); John Fitzgerald, *Big White Lie: Chinese Australians in White Australia* (Sydney: University of NSW Press, 2007) and *Awakening China: Politics, Class and Culture in the Nationalist Revolution* (Palo Alto, CA: Stanford University Press, 1998). For American history see: Erez Manela, 'Imagining Woodrow Wilson in Asia: Dreams of East–West Harmony and the Revolt against Empire in 1919', *American Historical Review* 111.5 (December 2006): 1327–1351.

11 Julia Martinez, 'Questioning White Australia: Unionism and Coloured Labor 1911–1937', *Labour History* 76 (May 1999): 1–19; Heather Goodall, 'Port Politics: Indian Seamen, Australian Unions and Indonesian Independence 1945–47', *Labour History* 94 (May 2008): 43–68. This is possibly because Russian or communist influences on interwar strike action have traditionally held more interest for labour historians.

12 Lake and Reynolds, *Drawing the Global Colour Line*, 38.

13 Gregor Benton, *Chinese Migrants and Internationalism: Forgotten Histories 1917–1945* (Oxford: Routledge, 2007), 91.

14 Wang Gungwu, 'Preface' to Gregor Benton, *Chinese Migrants and Internationalism*, xi.

15 The British brought Punjabi police to China from India as they considered these men superior police officers. Robert Bickers, *Empire Made Me: An Englishman Adrift in Shanghai* (London: Penguin Books, 2003), 32.

16 To the Director of the Pacific Branch, Prime Minister's Department, Melbourne, from Major General Commanding H.R.M. Troops in China (my emphasis). See also: 'Publications – Shanghai Publicity Bureau "News Bulletins"'; 'China – Anti-foreign movement'; 'External Affairs Department – China, Who's Who'; 'China – Foreign Concessions'.

17 'China – Foreign Concessions'.

18 Rebecca E. Karl, *Staging the World: Chinese Nationalism at the Turn of the Twentieth Century* (Durham, NC: Duke University Press, 2002), 90–112.

19 Rigby, *May 30th Movement*, 123. See also: Bickers, *Britain in China*, 35–36; S. A. Smith, *Revolution and the People in Russia and China* (London: Cambridge University Press, 2008).

20 Benton, *Chinese Migrants and Internationalism*, 3.

21 'Wu sha yun dong li liao, Historical Materials about "the May 30th Movement" 1925', Shanghai Municipal Archives (hereafter SMA) D2-02-14-154; D2-0-14-19; D2-0-2983-6.

22 'Trial of the Rioters at the Mixed Court', 10 September 1925 ('Wu sha yun dong li liao, Historical Materials about "the May 30th Movement" 1925'), SMA Q192-17-754, 16 34.

23 Ibid., 16, 34–35.

24 Ibid., 35. At the height of the May 30th Movement, people wearing foreign clothes were liable to have them splashed with acid, or to have insulting epithets written on pieces of paper secretly stuck to their backs. *North China Herald*, 13 June 1925.

25 SMA D2-0-2980-3.

26 'Trial of the Rioters at the Mixed Court'.
27 Bickers, *Britain in China*, 34.
28 'Trial of the Rioters at the Mixed Court'. See also: Robert Bickers, 'Shanghailanders: The Formation and Identity of the British Settler Community in Shanghai, 1843–1947', *Past and Present* 159 (May 1998): 161–211.
29 Eleanor Hinder papers, ML MSS 770, Box 20 (34).
30 'China – Labour Conference at Canton: Coloured Conference at Shanghai', NAA A981/4 CHIN 19.
31 Letter from Rex Phillips, 720 Avenue Joffre Shanghai, to His Family in Victoria, Australia, 15 March 1927, Papers of Rex, Clarence and Madge Phillips 1924–1926, National Library of Australia (NLA), MS 9942. See also: Sophie Loy-Wilson 'From Man of the British Empire to Proud Australian', *National Library News* 10 (July 2008): 11–14.
32 Harry Crittendon, Clerks Union, 1929, 'To Pinheaded Patriots, Jingoistic Dingoes, Collective Megalomaniacs, Hysterical Loyalists and Frenzied Flag-Flappers', George Waite papers, ML MSS 208, Box 2.
33 *Northern Standard*, 15 September 1921, quoted in Martinez, 'Coolies to Comrades', 300.
34 *One Big Union*, 2 February 1925.
35 Ibid.
36 *Seamen's Journal*, April 1925, 6.
37 Agatha Harrison correspondence, 1919–1925, Eleanor Hinder papers, ML MSS 277, Box 34.
38 Ibid. See also: John Host, *Victorian Labour History: Experience, Identity and the Politics of Representation* (London: Routledge, 1998).
39 'The Joint Committee of Shanghai's Women's Organization: Towards a Regulation of Child Labor in Shanghai', Bulletin No. 1, Eleanor Hinder papers, ML MSS 277, Box 34.
40 Jun Xing, *Baptized in the Fire of Revolution: The American Social Gospel and the YMCA in China 1919–1937* (Boston, MA: Harvard University Press, 1996), 56, 103.
41 'Industrial Conference', George Waite papers, ML MSS 208, Box 1 (3).
42 Ibid.
43 Jun Xing, *Baptized in the Fire of Revolution*.
44 Leoni Durrant, *Y.W.C.A. 1882–1982: Melbourne Pictorial History* (Melbourne: Ian Murray & Associates, 1982).
45 Agatha Harrison correspondence.
46 See: 'The Coles Girl', Eleanor Hinder papers, ML MSS 277, Box 2.
47 Agatha Harrison correspondence.
48 'Correspondence with the International Labor Organisation: Chinese Factory Act 1931', SMA DL 0111-0111-2228.
49 Sarah Paddle, 'For the China of the Future: Western Feminists, Colonisation and International Citizenship in China in the Inter-war Years', *Australian Feminist Studies* 16.36 (2001): 327–328.
50 Ma Zhang Lin, *Zu Jie Li de Shanghai* (Shanghai in Foreign Concessions), 240–254, SMA U1-6-111; Q1-5-518.
51 Eleanor Hinder papers, ML MSS 277, Box 20.
52 To the Honourable Stanley Melbourne Bruce from Trade Commissioners Office, Bureau of Foreign and Domestic Commerce, Shanghai, 23 April 1923, 'Trade Commissioners – China and the East', NAA A11804/1/1924/255. See also: 'China', NAA A981/4/CHIN 94, PART 1.
53 Frances Wheelhouse, *Eleanor Mary Hinder: An Australian Women's Social Welfare Work in China between the Wars* (Sydney: Wentworth Books, 1978), 25.

54 Translation of letter from Albert Thomas of the International Labour Offices to General McNaughton (Chairman of the Shanghai Municipal Council), League of Nations, 30 January 1938, ILO Correspondence, SMA D-0111-0111-2057.

55 Roland Marchland, *Creating the Corporate Soul: The Rise of Public Relations and Corporate Imagery in American Big Business* (Berkeley: University of California Press, 1986), 28–29.

56 Ibid., 274.

57 'The Long Hard Day in China', Eleanor Hinder papers, ML MSS 770, Box 20 (34).

58 Letter from Elizabeth Christman, National Women's Trade Union League of America, to the Shanghai Office of the YWCA, 12 November 1924, Eleanor Hinder papers, ML MSS 770, Box 20.

59 'The Long Hard Day in China'.

60 Petition addressed to Dame Adelaide Anderson from workers at the Lungwa cement factory.

61 'Threads: The Story of the Industrial Work of the Y.W.C.A in China', 1925, 7, Eleanor Hinder papers, ML MSS 770, Box 20.

62 'Report of the Industrial Committee 1926', 3, Eleanor Hinder papers, ML MSS 770, Box 20.

63 Ibid.

64 Extract from *Hansard*, March 1924, Eleanor Hinder papers, ML MSS 770, Box 20.

65 Ibid.

66 Angela Woollacott, *To Try Her Fortune in London: Australian Women, Colonialism and Modernity* (New York: Oxford University Press, 2001), 27.

67 'The Y.W.C.A. 189 Liverpool Street Sydney . . . Australia, Telephone, M 2858', Collection of pamphlets relating to activities of the Young Women's Christian Association, NLA, FERG/6466.

68 Factory Act Legislation, SMA 0111-0111-2231.

69 Translation of letter from Albert Thomas of the International Labour Offices to General McNaughton.

70 'Summary Note on Inspection of Factories', Shanghai, 17 November 1931, Albert Thomas Correspondence, SMA D-0111-0111-2106.

6 Trade Unionists, Patriots and Anticolonialists

If sound work can be initiated in these plastic days of Chinese industrial revolution it may give a new bent to their whole development.[1]

J. B. Taylor, Department of Economics, Peking University, 1920

Did Shanghai workers' stories find a sympathetic audience among Australian readers and, if so, how and why did this happen in the mid-1920s? While such 'sympathy' is hard to measure, union newspapers, labour leaders and Y pamphlets were clearly written for an implied reader – and the longevity and sweep of Shanghai storytelling across the mainstream press would indicate some sort of positive reception, or at least a sustained interest, within the wider community. By considering the interaction between left-leaning rhetoric about Shanghai and existing political realities, we can appreciate why this form of publicity may have been effective in promoting Australian trade unions in 1925.

Migration to the cities and a growth in manufacturing during the First World War meant that more Australians were working in factories than ever before by the mid-1920s.[2] In 1921 some 34 per cent of Sydney's population worked in manufacturing, mostly in the smoky crush of the inner city, in which factories (342 in one suburb alone) overshadowed boarding houses where migrants from the country made do in cramped quarters.[3] Richard Waterhouse argues that Australian workers were slower than their American counterparts to become acculturated to the rhythm of the modern factory, partly because, for many country migrants, the transition from rural to factory work was made very quickly, in the space of one generation.[4] Elsie Harrison remembered her stomach sinking in 1925 when at the age of fifteen she went to work in a stocking factory (Lustre Hosiery) in Darlinghurst because her father had lost his job as a council garbage collector: 'I said to a lady when I first got there – how long have you been here and she said "two years" and I said, "I hope I'm not here in two years time" . . . I was frightened.'[5] After three weeks' work her wages were cut from fourteen shillings and sixpence to thirteen shillings and thruppence, but she continued to work a forty-eight-hour week, paying ten shillings board to her parents every Sunday. 'It was the beginning of the Depression.'[6]

Figure 6.1 Packaging ice cream bars, Peters Ice Cream factory, Perth, *c.*1929.

Source: State Library of Western Australia.

Some Australian workplaces maintained genuinely appalling conditions that remained invisible to the wider public. In the shipping industry, sacks of cargo such as wheat, cement and potatoes weighing up to ninety-five kilograms were still mainly shifted on workers' backs (in cloth bags, not containers); coal and sulphur were moved by shovelling, causing eyes to stream; scratches were irritated by cement; soda ash caused nosebleeds; and castor-oil beans produced allergic reactions.[7] Animal hides arrived in Australia rotten and oozing with maggots, and unloading sugar attracted clouds of wasps. Technological advances were not necessarily designed to ease the burden. Melbourne hospitals treated frostbite in the heatwave of 1927 because men worked in freezer holds without protective clothing.[8] Cake-making machines in one Sydney factory caused 'dusted lung', a colloquial term for emphysema.[9]

It was textile work, however, that developed one of the worst reputations for workplace safety, and this was especially the case in Sydney. By the 1920s reports and photographs showing injuries received in textile factories were commonplace in Australian newspapers. As Jessie Viner, a former Joyce Brothers employee, told reporters:

Textile was upstairs. There were shafts and belts under each bench, these were uncovered. One girl had a section of her scalp pulled off when passing one of these belts. One girl's arm was caught as she was feeding bags into the printing machine . . . Most of us lost fingers, thumbs.[10]

Complaints of bad factory conditions coincided with a drop in pay. In what Alan Martin has termed an 'employer's offensive', further wage cuts and increased hours were introduced across urban factories.[11] The men and (an increasing number of) women doing this factory work were new audiences for union literature. A sense of slipping living standards led to reflections on an earlier era. As a 1925 Labor election pamphlet put it:

Years ago when there were no Unions, the condition of the workingman and woman were shocking . . . Women and children worked 14, 15 and 16 hours a day for from 5/- a week to 5/- a month – MERE SLAVES. Many people still remember the awful conditions under which people worked not so many years ago, and the poor wages they received.[12]

Considering the rapid decline in wages and conditions after 1918, it was not unreasonable for Australian factory workers to think worse was to come, and that workers on the other side of the world could hold up a mirror to this future. Shanghai's Zhabei factory district made such reflection a concrete reality. 'A 12 hour day *for children*' exclaimed one union poster entitled 'MURDER! An Indictment of Imperialism in China', which added:

The struggle of Chinese workers is a struggle against the perpetuation of cooliedom in China. If the [Chinese workers] fail NOW the Australian workers cannot escape from its repercussions in the shape of more unemployment and a lowering of the standard of labor conditions here.[13]

Resentment towards empire was growing in the Australian labour movement for other reasons as well. Britain was central to the Australian economy throughout the 1920s and 1930s and decisions made in its distant boardrooms, clubs and stock markets had major implications for Australia, its living standards and its urban make-up.[14] Unionists resented Australia's role as a 'vassal state' in the imperial economy as well as the number of migrants arriving from Britain each year as part of imperial migration programmes, who were 'taking jobs from unemployed Australians'. In 1921 alone Australia received 17,525 immigrants from Britain, a number that increased every year well into the Great Depression.[15] It was time, one Sydney labour speaker argued, for Australian workers to enter the global economy on equal terms.[16]

Images and stories from Zhabei became metaphors not only for 'factory life' but also for China's relations with Britain, and for venal empire trade more generally. The slave rhetoric implicit in Zhabei narratives expressed the grievances of Dominion states seemingly short-changed through preferential tariff arrangements with Britain. Dominion status was a characteristically ambiguous imperial invention that recognised various stages of self-government, while managing to convey overtones of continuing subordination, usually through economic policy.[17] Thus, testimonies and images from a Chinese factory district could expose the more subtle hierarchies of empire for an Australian audience, while at the same time collapsing race and class in an attack on British 'fat capital' in Asia. This hitching of national and racial identification to industrial dispute (British capital/Australian labour, Chinese workers/white bosses) enabled an aggressively parochial labour category, 'the fat boss', to become a stock figure in Pan-Asian independence movements. Here the British factory boss was a powerful device in the portrayal of a 'monster', conveying a gross power imbalance. Such a shift was not without gendered dimensions; Britain as 'fat' presented empire as 'effete, unmanly', while the colonial worker was 'taut, muscular, broad chested' and also Asian.[18]

Fruitfully tapping into the work of the Y, union publicity encouraged Australians to sympathise with the victims of Zhabei; to see their own workplace angst not as

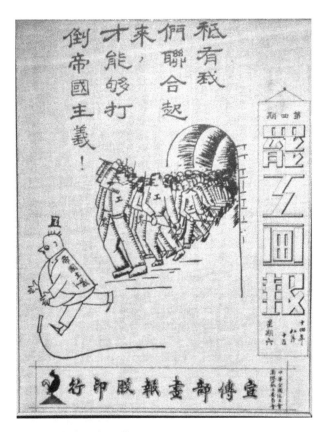

Figure 6.2 (continued)

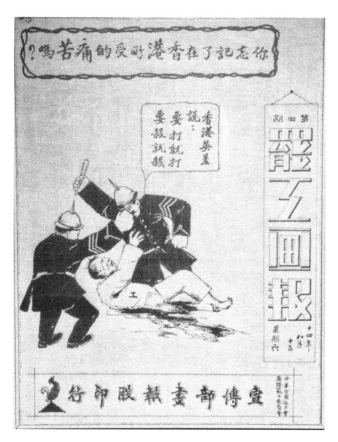

Figure 6.2 Sketch from *Hong Kong Strike Pictorial* encouraging workers to join the
1925 general strike in Hong Kong after the May 30th shootings.

Source: Hong Kong Museum collection.

the result of 'yellow competition' but as due to financial wheeling and dealing in
London at the expense of the Dominions. Shanghai was perfectly placed to
enunciate this sense of economic servitude. As of 1925 China existed in a state of
semi-colonial subservience, severely limited in the exercise of its sovereignty by a
net of unequal treaties and suffocating tariff arrangements with the major powers.
Chinese intellectuals, like their Indian counterparts, viewed their struggle for self-
determination as part of a broader revolt against imperialism.[19] China is 'an
international playground', wrote Yenching University Professor William Hung in
a pamphlet circulated in Australia, 'where for more than half a century all sorts of
games, all varieties of imperialism have been played'.[20] A country 'so controlled
and fettered' was 'obviously not' free. Britain should proceed to redress this 'great
historical wrong'.[21] If China was a 'playground' for the great powers, the

Dominions were the 'playthings' of British capital – or so argued *One Big Union* and the *Seamen's Journal*.[22] I do not wish to imply here that a majority of Australians wanted Britain to withdraw from East Asia in 1925 (this was patently not the case). What *will* become evident, however, is the impact of Chinese nationalism on the presentation of Australian political ideas and on the Labor Party, which chose – for a brief moment in 1925 – to support the liberation of China, while also arguing the case for an independent Australia.

'The *Brisbane* Affair'

We now arrive at 17 June 1925, when the Shanghai May 30th incident was woven into a Labor Party attack on conservative Australian Prime Minister Stanley Melbourne Bruce, and on the panoply of empire he had come to represent. As a Commonwealth intimate, Australia had lent England a navy cruiser, the HMAS *Brisbane*, as part of an exchange programme in 1924.[23] The *Brisbane* and its Australian crew had been assigned to the Admiralty's China Squadron and stationed on the China coast. From 30 May the ship was anchored in Shanghai, later moving to Hong Kong, and it was present when the fifty-two rioters in Shanghai were shot by SMP officers.[24] Whether or not Australian soldiers were implicated in the killing of Chinese civilians was unclear, but specifics became irrelevant. The affair inflated beyond its details, becoming a juncture, a 'questioning of empire', which saw trade unions and the Labor Party champion Chinese and Australian strikers as national heroes. The *Brisbane*'s presence in Shanghai and Hong Kong caused a diplomatic crisis as well as a public relations problem for Bruce, as it associated Australia with the British shootings and with the repression and violence that followed.

Prior to 17 June the Labor Party had been in the process of objecting to a bill legalising the deportation of unionists. Bruce had cancelled award wages for Australian sailors on 5 June and deregistered their union. British-born Tom Walsh led strikes in response. Having been imprisoned, he awaited transportation. Departing from their protests over deportation and strike crackdowns – but keenly sensing a connected story – Labor frontbenchers began to ask questions about what would become known as 'the *Brisbane* Affair'.[25] By allowing the *Brisbane* to be stationed in Chinese waters, Labor argued, Australia was interfering in an 'industrial dispute, attempting to suppress a strike', and abetting abhorrent 'British imperial schemes' in China. Labor Party leader Matthew Charlton spoke of the 'endeavour of the downtrodden Chinese to improve their condition; why should Australia contribute to [this] destruction of life?'[26] Frontbencher Frank Anstey proposed: 'Australians would be better engaged in supporting the rioters [in Shanghai] than in resisting them.' Billy Hughes asked: 'If white larrikins assaulted a Chinese cabinetmaker in Lonsdale Street, *would we allow that a Chinese warship that happened to be in port was entitled to intervene?*'[27] Queries as to the *Brisbane*'s precise role in the 'Shanghai Massacre' stretched over the following month, and the issue attached itself to Bruce until the elections of 1929. He was not helped by regular reports of more deaths in China at the hands of British troops.[28] The *Argus* and the *Sydney Morning Herald* swung their political coverage onto the affair and pressed larger questions. Was the 'writing on the wall for the British Empire'? Had Bruce's reverence for 'empire trade' and 'law and order' – such powerful and persuasive politics in the early 1920s – made Australia into a draconian state, deporting civilians, silencing dissent and abetting the shooting of protesters?[29] Billy Hughes made sure that Australian unions felt part of a unified Labor offensive. On his urging, the Australian Workers Union (AWU) petitioned Bruce: 'The AWU representing 140,000 organised workers in Australia views with alarm the happenings in China and demands that the Federal government shall not embroil Australians in Imperialistic Warfare in defense of capitalistic concessions in China.'[30]

Hughes, a passionate devotee of the White Australia Policy and of white race patriotism, was an unlikely conduit for Chinese nationalism in Australia. In 1919 he had been instrumental in keeping a 'racial equality' clause out of the Treaty of Versailles.[31] But Hughes had been the recipient of Y publicity since 1923, and his exposure to its work in China is one possible explanation for his new sympathies. Whatever other motivations he may have had, Hughes could hardly have failed to appreciate the opportunity now at his feet. Intruding in Chinese waters, looming over treaty port docklands and displaying guns and cannon on its decks, the *Brisbane* was spoken of as resembling the British battleship *Dreadnought*, an Anglo-Australian affront to Chinese sovereignty, space and freedom.[32] Like the navy cruisers anchored at Australian wharves during recent seamen's strikes, the HMAS *Brisbane* was a 'deterrent to free speech', an 'enemy of the people'. What Hughes attacked was not the *Brisbane* or its crew per se, but the indiscriminate and excessive *militancy* it had come to represent, a militancy on clear display as Bruce's government troops clashed with unionists on Australian wharves, in the city streets and at the coal mines.

Labor and union leaders produced a way of thinking about Australia's historical situation in 1925 from within an anticolonial frame that they pieced together from observing, and linking Australian strike action to, events in China. These new visions of cross-colonial solidarity were explicitly intended to subvert arguments that placed empire loyalty before Australia's national and regional self-interest. That Bruce took Labor's arguments seriously is evidenced by the flurry of secret telegrams that shot between London and Melbourne over the following months. On 19 June the Australian Governor General cabled London: 'My Prime Minister desirous of being kept fully informed of any fresh developments in Chinese situation. He also desires to be notified of any developments in movement of HMAS *Brisbane*.'[33] The Secretary for Dominion Affairs responded from London, but the answer was not considered sufficient and, on 24 June, Bruce sent another telegram:

> In the event of the China Squadron being employed in relation to any action taken by the powers in relation to the disturbances in China a situation of great importance is created in view of 'Brisbane' being included in squadron and under command of British admiral.[34]

London replied that Australia had 'misunderstood' the agreement: 'I am in some doubt whether the attitude of my government . . . [has] been fully appreciated.'[35] In yet more telegrams sent in early July, Bruce demanded to be kept better informed of Britain's plans in Asia through 'proper channels of communication, and proper consultation'.[36] Lord Amery agreed to an inquiry into the *Brisbane*'s role on and after 30 May 1925, but the report was dragged through bureaucracy and Bruce did not receive the results until late in 1926. They were perfunctory: 'Whilst at Hong Kong H.M.A.S. Brisbane was employed on Naval and military essentials, which it was necessary to maintain owing to the strike of Chinese employed by the Navy and Army.'[37]

Almost without exception, commentary on the *Brisbane* Affair was conspicuous in assuming support on behalf of Australians for Shanghai's strikers. Clearly, Labor and union leaders at the time felt that popular feeling opposing the May 30th shootings was strong. This sentiment was put to broader rhetorical use during what Billie Oliver has called 'the bleakest years of Australian unionism', as the Bruce government introduced yet more anti-union legislation, such as the Beeby Award, the Transport Workers Act (or 'Dog-Collar Act') and, finally, an attempt to ban wage arbitration in 1929.[38] Debate over the *Brisbane* Affair gave way to the chaos of a maritime strike that crippled the country in mid-1925. At the beginning of August, the wage of a British seaman was cut by 10 per cent, beginning a seamen's strike across the empire which saw over 4,000 men refuse to set sail. As punishment their clothes and all their other possessions were confiscated upon leaving the ships.[39] Via the Australian government-owned Commonwealth Shipping Line, the strike spread to Perth, Melbourne, Sydney, New Zealand, South Africa and Hong Kong. Conditions on Commonwealth boats were so bad that the line had been given the pseudonym of 'the floating slum'.[40] The strike extended in Australia from 19 August to 28 November, a total of 102 days.[41] On 20 August over 1,000 seafarers from Australia and around the empire attended a mass meeting at the Communist Hall in Sydney and voted to strike in all Australian ports until the £1 cut was restored.[42]

Wages were not the only source of resentment. Sailors wanted to change the way men were chosen for work when ships came into harbour. Free selection pickups 'were a humiliating scene. Men, numbering far in excess of the number required, often literally stand before the picker appealing with eloquent eyes and gestures to be chosen for the job. It is the nearest approach in modern times to the slave market of old.'[43] In early May 1925, Queensland unionists had abolished 'free standing', but shipping companies had responded by refusing to use their ports and the Bruce government had ruled in favour of the companies. Imperial loyalty had been deployed successfully by employers' organisations during the 'free standing' dispute (also known as the Cairns Rotary strike), linking perfectly with the pro-British policies of the Bruce–Page governments and mobilising a jingoistic race-patriotism that divided loyal empire employers from traitorous strikers.[44] This rhetoric had been difficult for unions to counter, as empire trade and the Commonwealth Shipping Line had become bywords for Britishness and the strikers synonymous with 'communists'.[45] But, as of August, 'empire rhetoric' had lost its traction, unions were united on the 'Shanghai issue' and Bruce's popularity was beginning to wane. In 1929 he became the first Australian prime minister to lose his seat at a Federal election.

As the seamen's strike stretched on, Labor and union pamphlets and posters portrayed Bruce as synonymous with British shipping interests, an association that firmly stuck when he sold the Commonwealth Shipping Line to the British Baron Kylsant for £7,500,000. Bruce's family firm, Paterson Laing & Bruce, was an importer whose goods were often delayed by waterside industrial action. He also held shares in a British shipping company, the profits of which might be reduced by wharf action in Australia.[46] He began to be caricatured in Labor publicity; in one example he is depicted standing next to large boats, dressed in an exaggerated suit, tails and monocle, stopping 'Labor' from loading 'eggs, wheat, fruit, butter' on deck, declaring airily that: 'The government stands steadfastly for loyalty to the throne.' Meanwhile, the King, in coronation robes and furs, yells across the bow: 'Come on Aussie, if you want your produce shifted, you'll have to pay combine rates.'[47] Other posters showed titanic cruisers disgorging swarms of British unemployed onto Australian wharves (labelled 'Bruce's Army'), while Australian workers streamed dejectedly out of a 'closed factory'.[48] In early 1925 Bruce had exploited positive associations in the electorate between the National Party and an organic vision of the British Empire:

> To-day Australia is being challenged by the organized workers. They seek to disrupt the Empire. They are fomenting trouble in trade and industry. They must be taught to uphold the law. The Nationalists will enforce order amongst these elements.[49]

Such a position was difficult to defend against the backdrop of the Shanghai incident. 'Law and order' became a less palatable policy once the ramifications of 'upholding the law' were played out in the form of civilian deaths in China. While Australian strikes did not result in deliberate government shootings, militarism persisted. In 1926 a striker, and Gallipoli veteran, was shot by a stray police bullet in Perth, and in 1928 seven bombs were set off on the Melbourne wharves and at the houses of prominent shipowners, injuring fifteen bystanders.[50]

What does it all mean in 'these plastic days'?

As we have seen, global linkages were increasingly phrased not in the language of empire, but in the language of a shared oppression under imperial capitalism. This language divorced 'imperialism' from its association with civilisation, benevolence and Britishness – depicting instead an imperialism located in industrialising areas of China. In these locations, empire was embodied in the crude language of a factory manager ('Children's hands do the work better') and the angry banners and graffiti of native protests ('Remember the May massacre! Down with Capitalism! Down with the British!'). By giving one side of empire prominence in Australian press and public debates, union leaders effectively undermined the moral platform of empire unity from which conservative leaders explained and justified their policies.

Shanghai became, for some Australian unionists, a replica of England in the early years of the Industrial Revolution. Therefore, improving the lives of Chinese workers was a rare chance to 'civilise capitalism' at its inception. So argued J. B. Taylor, a Peking University Professor of Economics. He stated: 'If sound work can be initiated in these plastic days of Chinese industrial revolution it may give a new bent to their whole development.'[51] Here was a way to avoid the human cost of early industrialism in Europe, while also making solid the oft-lauded ideals of empire: British justice, civilisation, progress and the protection of human dignity. But when it was discovered that many of the worst factories were actually British-owned, empire was thrown into a paradox; imperial capitalism conceived as salvation and uplift had brought enslavement – captured in photographs, testimonies and the shocked accounts of foreign journalists and missionaries. In these accounts, the scalps of young women were torn from their heads as they dozed against looms in sixteen-hour shifts, while the hands of young children were mangled in poorly maintained machinery – all under the watch of British factory managers. Through Shanghai, Australian unionists could conjure the world before unions and project its horrors graphically and ominously onto a hypothetical Australian future, demonstrating 'what it will be like' if Bruce succeeded in his attempts to de-unionise Australian workplaces.

Subverting the logics of 'empire marketing', Australian trade unions revealed the ways in which this Britishness was both a local and a global invention, formed betwixt Shanghai and Sydney, wharves and factories, and dependent on both places for the maintenance of an identity and a purpose. Britishness encompassed English laws and liberty, but also the display of these laws and liberties at the raw edges of empire's territorial reach. Britons who transgressed these laws in view of the international community tarnished the 'quality' and claims of British liberty and, therefore, the potency of Britishness as a public relations tool. Therefore, an 'incident' in Shanghai could alter the fabric of trade union publicity in Sydney, Fremantle or Brisbane, and the use of force on Australian or Chinese protesters could always be read as a statement about empire's legitimacy. Australia may have been, as Curran and Ward argue, first and foremost a British nation in the interwar years, but this was a Britishness literally and figuratively tangled up in the liberation of Asia.[52]

Australian Professor J. Merle Davis was shipbound in 1925, travelling Australasia on a research grant from the Institute of Pacific Relations. He observed the fallout from Shanghai's May 30th incident with something like psychic shock:

> I have met numerous pessimists on this trip who talk of Britain's declining power. Some of her own people say she is doomed. Others affirm that all western civilization is a sinking ship and still others claim that Asiatic industrial and commercial development is putting the 'hand-writing on the wall'.[53]

Merle himself felt pulled towards his and Australia's British origin. While it was true that developments in the Far East were bound to change history and 'swing the centre of world affairs more and more into the Pacific', he saw no great cause for alarm as long as 'Great Britain's overseas Dominions cherish her best traditions, are true to her interests and preserve their fine loyalty'. And, after all, 'the British ship of state has a great anchor to windward in the economic storm that is breaking on her from out of the East'. Still, Merle, along with other Australian observers, sensed a subtle, indisputable shift of powers:

> The whole racial process in the Pacific seems glacier like, vast cosmic forces moving slowly and irresistibly. But I see no solution and less satisfaction in lying down and letting ourselves be flattened out. It seems to me that it is up to human courage and intelligence to face these glacier-like forces and devise new channels into which they can be diverted and controlled and eventually made to serve human ends.[54]

Whether the death of a lone textile worker such as Gu Zhenghong at the hands of a factory guard and the presence of the *Brisbane* in Shanghai during the killings that followed aided the force of such a glacier was incidental. The May 30th massacre and the affinity some Australians felt with its victims seemed to be part of a slow, rolling and inevitable decline, a parting of water as allegorical ships and currents – once so vital in the maintenance of British power – strained the very connections their symbolism and utility had once helped create.

The globalisation of trade union publicity meant overseas street and strike violence was read in new ways, finding resonances and papering over differences (factional, racial, geographic). Photography and the quickening beat of communication made protests and strike action in far-flung places easier to access – more emotive, more relevant, somehow more 'shared'. The behaviour of Europeans in 1920s Shanghai, 'that hotbed of the Anti-Foreign movement in Asia', had unforeseen and unpredictable meanings for the labour movement in Australia, and for the ways unionism was made appealing to a newly urbanised workforce.[55] Reflecting on May 30th from an Australian perspective illustrates the normative and political significance of indigenous self-determination movements throughout the twentieth century, at a time when media technologies and political cultures – be they communist, capitalist or nationalist – were redrawing and collapsing the bonds of empire.

The communist/capitalist divide had a relational impact on popular understandings of racial difference in Australasia, and especially on the link between colonialism and civilisation. British factory managers benefiting from the work of children, women breastfeeding while posted at machines, the beheading of Shanghai union officials and the turning of guns and battleships on May 30th protesters did not present a 'civilised' face for empire. In the struggle to maintain empire, Britain was corrupting Britishness as a progressive force for the greater good, thereby diffusing the arguments of pro-British leaders in the Dominions. This was a battle over how industrialism should proceed in the colonies, and the proper role of British governance in this process. Through such an imaginary, a new ideal of Chinese 'worker' was born – a worker not so much in competition with Australians as in league with them, both oppressed, as it were, by 'the British race'. Trade union sympathy for Shanghai shows that Asia was vital not only in constituting Australian imperial identities, but also in their unmaking.

Notes

1 J. B. Taylor, Department of Economics, Peking University, 14 October 1920, Eleanor Hinder papers 1897–1963, Mitchell Library (ML) MSS 770, Box 20 (34).
2 Peter Spearitt, *Sydney's Century: A History* (Sydney: University of NSW Press, 2000), especially 'The Suburbanisation of Work', 109–131.
3 Ibid., 112.
4 Richard Waterhouse, *Private Pleasures, Public Leisure: A History of Australian Popular Culture since 1788* (Melbourne: Longman, 1995), 95.
5 Elsie Harrison interviewed by Janet Morris, Paddington Oral History Project, ML CY MLOH 435/61-62.
6 Ibid.
7 Margo Beasley, *Wharfies: A History of the Waterside Workers' Federation of Australia* (Sydney: Halstead Press, 1996), 76–77. See also: M. Tull, 'Blood on the Cargo: Cargo Handling and Working Conditions on the Waterfront at Fremantle 1900–1939', *Labour History* 52 (May 1987): 19.
8 Rupert Lockwood, *Ship to Shore: A History of Melbourne's Waterfront and Its Union Struggles* (Sydney: Hale & Iremonger, 1990), 31–35, 223–230.
9 Carolyn Polizzotto, *The Factory Floor: A Visual and Oral Record* (Fremantle: Fremantle Arts Centre Press, 1988), 200.
10 Ibid., 62, 121, 128.
11 Alan Martin, 'The Politics of the Depression', in Robert Manne (ed.) *The Australian Century: Political Struggles in the Building of a Nation* (Melbourne: Text Publishing, 1999), 80–119.
12 'Deportation: Bill to Crush Trade Unionism', in *Notes and Guides for Labor Speakers* (Sydney: The Worker Trade Union Print, 1925), 9.
13 'Murder! An Indictment of Imperialism in China', published by the Communist Party of Great Britain (London, 1925). Distributed by M. H. Ellis in Australia, National Library of Australia, MHE 8:2.
14 Erik Eklund, *Steel Town: The Making and Breaking of Port Kembla* (Carlton: Melbourne University Press, 2003), 13.
15 Ibid., 14.
16 'Newspaper Cuttings', George Waite papers, ML MS 208, Box 1.
17 A. G. Hopkins, 'Rethinking Decolonization', *Past and Present* 200.1 (2008): 212.
18 Nick Dyrenfurth and Marion Quartly, 'Fat Man v "The People": Labor Intellectuals and the Making of Oppositional Identities 1890–1901', *Labour History* 92 (May 2007): 31–56.
19 Erez Manela, 'Imagining Woodrow Wilson in Asia: Dreams of East–West Harmony and the Revolt against Empire in 1919', *American Historical Review* 111.5 (December 2006): 4. Imperialist countries imposed a series of unequal treaties that opened China to trade by, among other methods, denying China the ability to restrict imports by raising tariffs. When China recovered tariff autonomy in the late 1920s, it immediately imposed tariffs to restrict market access. The tariff rate of 1934 was seven times the pre-1929 rate. See: Karl Gerth, *China Made: Consumer Culture and the Creation of the Nation* (Boston, MA: Harvard University Press, 2003), 1–16.

20 Address on 'Nationalist China', 113th New York luncheon discussion, Foreign Policy Institute, 2 February 1929, featuring William Hung, Arthur N. Holcomb and David Z. T. Yui, New York Periodical Press (New York, 1929), 5. See: 'China – Press', NAA A981/4/CHIN 80 PART 2.

21 Ibid.

22 'Newspaper Cuttings', George Waite papers.

23 'China Delegation 1925, Position of H.M.A.S. Brisbane', Commonwealth of Australia, Governor General's Office, NAA A6661/1/297. See also: 'China – Labour', NAA A198/4/CHIN71.

24 'The Brisbane', *The Argus*, 20 January 1927. For a history of British naval intervention in China see: John Fitzgerald, *Awakening China: Politics, Class and Culture in the Nationalist Revolution* (Palo Alto, CA: Stanford University Press, 1998), 109–114. Fitzgerald notes that the British navy had long signified British civilisation and racial superiority in Asia: 'As Daniel Defoe's Robinson Crusoe declared, "What are their ports, supplied with a few junks and barks, to our navigation, our merchant fleets, our large and powerful navies?"'

25 'The Brisbane'.

26 See: Bobbie Oliver, 'Back from the Brink 1917–29', in John Faulkner and Stuart Macintyre (eds.) *True Believers: The Story of the Australian Labor Party* (Sydney: Allen & Unwin, 2001), 47–60.

27 My emphasis. 'China Delegation 1925, Position of H.M.A.S. Brisbane'; 'The Brisbane'. See also: 'China – Labour'.

28 To the Director of the Pacific Branch, Prime Minister's Department, Melbourne, from Major General Commanding HRM Troops in China, 'China Command Intelligence Diary for June 1925', Secret JG 533/5, NAA A10915/1/1. See also: 'Publications – Shanghai Publicity Bureau "News Bulletins"', NAA A981/PUB78; 'China – Anti-foreign Movement', NAA A981/4 CHIN 48; 'China – Foreign Concessions', NAA A981/4 CHIN 61.

29 'The Case of the H.M.A.S. Brisbane' and other newspaper cuttings, 'China Delegation 1925, Position of H.M.A.S. Brisbane'.

30 Letter to the Secretary, Prime Minister of Australia, Commonwealth Offices, from John Barnes, President of the Australian Workers Union, 28 January 1926, 'China', NAA A981/4/CHIN 94.

31 Marilyn Lake and Henry Reynolds, *Drawing the Global Colour Line: White Men's Countries and the Question of Racial Equality* (Melbourne: Melbourne University Press, 2008), 295–296, 310.

32 David Z. T. Yui, 'Presence of Foreign Ships and Gunboats: China Does Not Exist Mainly for Foreign Trade and Exploitations', in 'China and the World', *Institute of Pacific Relations News Bulletin* (November 1927), 7.

33 Secret: Decode of Cabled Telegram Dispatched by His Excellency the Governor General to the Secretary of State for Dominion Affairs, 6 July 1925, 7:30pm, 'China Delegation 1925, Position of H.M.A.S. Brisbane'.

34 Ibid.

35 Ibid.

36 Memorandum for the Official Secretary of the Governor General, Melbourne, 3 July 1925, 'China Delegation 1925, Position of H.M.A.S. Brisbane'.

37 'Work Done by H.M.A.S. Brisbane in Connection with Local Disturbance in China', 'China Delegation 1925, Position of H.M.A.S. Brisbane'.

38 Oliver, 'Back from the Brink', 7–60; Beasley, *Wharfies*, 83.

39 Ibid., 1–2.

40 *The Reverend F.E. Maynard Defends the Strike of the British Seamen* (Brisbane: Standard Press Union Label, 1925), 7.

41 Ibid., 51.

42 *The Argus*, 22 August 1925.

43 'Bowan Branch Leaflet', Waterside Workers Federation Holdings, ML Q331.87/W.
44 Alan Martin, 'The Politics of the Depression'.
45 Beasley, *Wharfies*, 69.
46 Lockwood, *Ship to Shore*, 202.
47 'At the Mercy of Kylsant and Inchape', Voltaire Molesworth papers 1901–1931, ML MSS 398, Box 2.
48 Ibid., 'Bruce's Army: Unemployed, Vote Labor!'.
49 Ibid., 'Bruce Plays a Dangerous Game'.
50 Beasley, *Wharfies*, 88.
51 Letter from J. B. Taylor, Peking University, Department of Economics, to Agatha Harrison, 14 October 1920, Eleanor Hinder papers, ML MSS 277, Box 34.
52 Stuart Ward and James Curran, *The Unknown Nation: Australia after Empire* (Carlton: Melbourne University Press, 2010), 13. See also: Neville Kirk, '"Australians for Australia": The Right, the Labor Party and Contested Loyalties to Nation and Empire in Australia 1917 to the Early 1930s', *Labour History* 91 (November 2006): 95–111.
53 J. Merle Davis, *Institute of Pacific Relations News Bulletin* (16 October 1926), 8.
54 Ibid.
55 Ibid.

Conclusion

Geoffrey Blainey suggested in the 1960s how distance shaped Australian history, but now connection and proximity claim as much attention.[1]

Alison Bashford and Stuart Macintyre, 'Introduction',
The Cambridge History of Australia (2013)

All international tension centres in Shanghai. China has but become for the time being a conspicuous stage for the great drama in racial relationships which we believe is being enacted in one form or another all around the world.

YWCA China pamphlet *Threads* (1925)

The history of Australia's encounters with China is usually told through two key moments: Chinese miners coming to Australia during the gold rushes and Australian diplomats visiting China to re-establish ties with Australia's newly powerful neighbour at the end of the Cold War.[2] Gough Whitlam's 1972 trip to Peking, two months before that of President Nixon, is the subject of at least two books in recent years and numerous newspaper articles.[3] Such a foundational history is convenient, as it provides a redemptive narrative for Australian politics, a way to throw off the long shadow of White Australia and usher in a new era of Australia–China friendship.

This is what Antoinette Burton means when she says that when we visualise the work individuals or people do to move accounts of world history forward, we see a dotted landscape where the landscape itself is not just a horizon but marks the ground of historical visibility, the threshold to which legitimate subjects of all kinds must rise in order to be recognised and cited as such.[4] In Sino-Australian relationships, two events and two groups of men have marked this dotted landscape – gold-rush era migrants moving to white settler societies and post-Cold War warriors opening up China to capitalism and Western diplomacy.

This book suggests we take a different way in, that this narrative looks thin if we look beyond traditional sites of political power for our explanations of historical change. When we look closely at alternative sites – to the archives of Chinese Australian families, to Shanghai Municipal Police reports, to letters shuttling between missionaries, anticolonialists and internationalists – we discover that Sino-Australian migration moved both ways. White Australian women and their

Eurasian children populated the nineteenth-century Chinese countryside, as the wives of returned Chinese miners.[5] Chinese Australian families, their lives tied to both the Pearl River Delta and the New South Wales hinterland, were at the vanguard of Shanghai modernity as returned overseas Chinese. In later periods, China's ports attracted Australia's economic migrants during the Great Depression, and China's labour movement inspired Australian unionists. Australian internationalist women clustered in Shanghai to advocate for the universal rights of women and children, using the plight of Chinese female factory workers as the key examples to support these campaigns.

Meanwhile, in Australia, Chinese gold miners were far from the marginalised victims of Australian racism so common in Australian school textbooks – they were, as Marilyn Lake has shown, co-colonists, settling in Australia, owning land, exploiting indigenous labour, and writing political pamphlets advocating for universal human rights and racial equality. Later generations were passionate anticolonial advocates who joined forces with Australian internationalists in their condemnation of European colonialism in China, and in Asia more broadly. So, in between the two canonical events so often used to map Australia's shared history with China are myriad other dots in the landscape, dots which allow us to revisit poorly understood connections across the South China Sea – through war, capital and migration; through bodies that only become visible if we look beyond traditional spaces of politics to tell our stories.

***

In the early 1990s Chinese historians in Shanghai began a series of oral history interviews with residents who had lived in the city in the 1920s and 1930s.[6] They wandered up high-rise apartments, into the Art Deco homes of the old French Concession, now owned by China's rich, and into decrepit apartment blocks, known locally as 'boat houses' due to their cramped and damp conditions, which had, after the nationalisation of property under the communists post-1949, housed up to four families in one room.[7] In one of these, they met ninety-five-year-old Daisy Kwok, whose life we charted at the beginning of this book. The interview that they conducted with her was published in Mandarin in *Shanghai de Feng Hua Xue Yue* (Shanghai Memorabilia) in 2008.[8]

Daisy's story illustrates the central concerns of this book. Her life story, as told to Chinese historians, demonstrates how the archival trails left behind by Australians in Shanghai take on dense cultural meanings in ways that are productive for historians. Daisy was ethnically Chinese but born and raised in Australia. She went to Shanghai from Sydney in 1917 in her teens. She spoke no Chinese upon arrival in China, having only heard snatches of the language in Sydney's Chinatown, or spoken by her grandfather's shopworkers. Her parents – descendants of gold miners from different parts of south China – spoke in English. She arrived in Shanghai after her grandfather's Wing On Company opened a department store on the water's edge. The family lived in mansions and travelled to Europe once a year. Daisy rode horses, wore silk and fox fur. In Australia, Wing On products (bolts of cloth, tins of ginger, produced in factories in the Zhabei district) were packed into trains and vans and distributed to the most remote country towns to sit on the shelves of general stores.[9]

After her marriage Daisy owned and worked in a clothing shop, where she sold high-end fashion and also exported dresses to Australia. Meanwhile, hearing that the communists might win the Civil War with the Nationalists, her husband buried a revolver under the tree in their front yard. Someone saw the burial. When the communists did indeed take over the city, Daisy's husband was led away to prison, where he died. Daisy herself was sent to a re-education camp for 'enemies of the people'.[10] During humiliation sessions at the camp in the 1950s she wore a dunce cap and placard with characters on it she could not read, accused of crimes she could not decipher, for her Chinese was still rudimentary; she had run her business mostly in English.[11] Her Australian roots and her links with Wing On Department Store aligned her with 'capitalist imperialists' and singled her out for harsh punishment. In the 1980s Australian descendants of Daisy's family, the Kwoks, met for reunions and raised money for a Chinese Australian history museum in Melbourne, where her family's story featured among other stories of successful Chinese Australian trading families.

Daisy's association with Sino-Australian relations was written into Chinese and Australian national narratives in particular ways. In Australia, her story is bound up with the restrictions placed on Chinese Australian business under the White Australia Policy.[12] In Chinese histories of Shanghai, her life and her connection to the Wing On retail empire are associated with a perceived Chinese Australian collusion with Western capitalism and imperialism during the treaty port era.[13] These reactions to Chinese Australian commercial practices tell us much about the strange ground between migration and cultural change and the ways in which Australians in Shanghai embodied this cultural change.

This book has used the lives of Australians in Shanghai to study processes that shaped the emergence of colonial modernity in Australia and China in the twentieth century. The writings of these Australians in Shanghai and the archives of the institutions for which they worked reveal a more dynamic and geographically expansive view of this period than has previously been documented in Australian scholarship. Further, they demonstrate the need to position Australia in a transnational geography that takes into account the messiness of the cultural and economic links binding Australia to the Asian region and to global networks. They show that individuals' aspirations for mobility in a newly federated settler society often came into conflict with nation- and empire-building policies such as rural settlement, immigration law, tariff restrictions, industrial arbitration and empire trade agreements. Following mobile Australians into factories and rural towns, on board boats bound for Shanghai, into Chinese shops and up and down the elevators of department stores provides a counterpoint to national histories that depict Australian society in the interwar years as inward-looking and isolated. This variegated material is bound together by Australians in Shanghai. I have shown how Australians in the twentieth century translated ideologies of industrial efficiency and mass democracy into their everyday interactions and personal aspirations both at home and at work. I have also traced the ways in which the Great Depression encouraged some Australians to engage with Asia in new ways. This shift can be viewed at a number of levels: through the migration of Australians to interwar Shanghai to look for work or through the response of the Australian union movement to Chinese anticolonialism. Information flows made possible by the YWCA between Australia and China changed the forms through which Australian unions promoted industrial action. Australian traders in Shanghai became part of Chinese conceptions of European imperialism. The point is not that Australian communities in Shanghai were the cause of this engagement, but rather that it allows us to view hitherto unexamined Australian and Asian connections and that, when we do so, assumptions about Australia's isolation from Asia during this period are problematised. I do not offer a comprehensive study of these connections but I do suggest that they are significant.

Furthermore, researching Australians in Shanghai consistently leads to non-English language archives. What can historians make of these sources? Such sources have not featured in studies of Australian 'modernity', although historians of nineteenth-century Australia have long noted the role of Asian migration on the Australian 'frontier' or in the formation of white, working-class identity in settler colonies. These disparate archives do not fit easily into one historiographical field. Rather, they suggest productive connections between fields such as urban history, economic history, colonial history and transnational history.

If we come into Sino-Australian history at an economic register, we uncover a long history of economic interconnections and China–Australia trade relations that are rarely acknowledged in Australian national histories. And if we do this, if we take economic archives seriously, we bring valuable Chinese language sources about Australia into view. In my current research I am working towards realigning the way we periodise this history, and pay attention to sources and actors that demonstrated connections outside of these dominant historical markers. The economic shifts were intimately tied to global and regional trade and commodity chains. Commercial publications such as *Rydge's Business Journal* urged their readers to travel door-to-door, or town-to-town as well as port-to-port, in the Eastern markets. Studying the awkward and uneven ways in which individuals tried to apply these ideas to their personal and professional lives uncovers how individual aspiration motivated transcolonial connections, forging pathways sometimes counter to the wishes of national policymakers.

Notes

1   Alison Bashford and Stuart Macintyre, 'Introduction', in Alison Bashford and Stuart Macintyre (eds.) *The Cambridge History of Australia, Volume 1: Indigenous and Colonial Australia* (New York: Cambridge University Press, 2013), 5.
2   See for example: Shirley Fitzgerald, *Red Tape Golden Scissors: The Story of Sydney's Chinese* (Sydney: State Library of NSW Press, 1996), especially chapter 5 'Tightening the Screws', 124–155; Keir Reeves and Jan Tsen Khoo (eds.) 'Special Issue: Chinese Australian History', *Australian Historical Studies* 42.1 (March 2011).

3 Billy Griffiths, *The China Breakthrough: Whitlam in the Middle Kingdom, 1971* (Melbourne: Monash University Press, 2012); Stephen Fitzgerald, *Comrade Ambassador: Whitlam's Beijing Envoy* (Melbourne: Melbourne University Press, 2015).
4 Antoinette Burton, 'The Body in/as World History', in Douglas Northrup (ed.) *A Companion to World History* (London: Wiley-Blackwell, 2012), 279.
5 Kate Bagnall, 'Rewriting the History of Chinese Families in Nineteenth-Century Australia', *Australian Historical Studies* 42.1 (March 2011): 62–77.
6 Dong Feng Pei (ed.) *Shanghai de Feng Hua Xue Yue* (Shanghai Memorabilia) (Shanghai: Shanghai Historical Press, 2008), 307–320.
7 Ibid., 307.
8 Ibid., 307–320.
9 Data on this trade is lacking. Indeed, statistical information on the movement of individuals and commodities between Australia and Asia in the interwar period has fallen outside the bounds of this book and constitutes an area of future research.
10 'Humanities Salon: Cities – Shanghai: Colonialism, Cosmopolitanism and Chinese Modernity', Dr Yiyan Wang and Dr Yi Zheng in conversation with Professor David Goodman, 30 September 2010, Sydney Law School Foyer, University of Sydney.
11 Wing On Company files, Shanghai Municipal Archives, Q223-2-43, Q225-2-79, Q225-3-21, Q225-3-22, Q225-3-23, Q225-3-26.
12 Janice Wilton, 'Chinese Stores in Rural Australia', in Kerrie K. Macpherson (ed.) *Asian Department Stores* (Surrey: Curzon, 1998), 90–113; Fitzgerald, *Red Tape Golden Scissors*, especially chapter 5 'Tightening the Screws', 124–155; C. F. Young, *The New Gold Mountain: The Chinese in Australia* (Richmond, British Columbia: Mitchell Press, 1978), especially chapter 2 'Chinese Labouring Classes and Merchants', 35–59. See also: Sophie Loy-Wilson, 'Peanuts and Publicists: "Letting Australian Friends know the Chinese Side of the Story" in Interwar Sydney', *History Australia* 6.1 (2009): 1–20; 'Trouble in White Australia', Honours Thesis, University of Sydney, 2006.
13 Dong Feng Pei (ed.) *Shanghai de Feng Hua Xue Yue*, 307–320; 'Humanities Salon: Cities – Shanghai: Colonialism, Cosmopolitanism and Chinese Modernity'.

Index

For Product Safety Concerns and Information please contact our EU
representative GPSR@taylorandfrancis.com
Taylor & Francis Verlag GmbH, Kaufingerstraße 24, 80331 München, Germany

www.ingramcontent.com/pod-product-compliance
Ingram Content Group UK Ltd.
Pitfield, Milton Keynes, MK11 3LW, UK
UKHW020947180425
457613UK00019B/573